D1475166

A Commentary on

REVELATION

The Grand Finale

A Commentary on

REVELATION

The Grand Finale

CHARLES LEE FEINBERG

BMH BOOKS

P.O. Box 544
Winona Lake, Indiana 46590

ISBN: 0-88469-162-4

Copyright 1985 by Charles Fee Feinberg

First Printing, February 1985
BMH Books
Winona Lake, Indiana

Printed in U.S.A.

TO
OUR CHILDREN
AND
GRANDCHILDREN
THIS VOLUME IS DEDICATED
WITH LOVE
* * *

TABLE OF CONTENTS

PREFACE

Judging from the great number of commentaries and other works on the Book of Revelation, it is not difficult to see that the book has always held a paramount place in the thinking and esteem of Bible students and scholars. It is without cavil the capstone of the Bible, an endless source of comfort to the household of faith. Admittedly, no writer on this inestimable volume can or should claim he has the final word on this book of Scripture. But this is no reason either to neglect its glorious message or engage in fantastic flights of the imagination. We all do well to realize it is God's final unveiling of the glories of His blessed Son. Our focus must ever be on Him in this Grand Finale. The book is an incomparable Christology in itself.

It is always a joy to give thanks for the work of the publishing staff. My gratitude is here expressed also to Miss Shirley Shively, my competent and faithful secretary, who was always available when needed. For the intelligence, patience, and help in many ways of my dear wife, it is impossible adequately to express my genuine appreciation.

May the Lord abundantly bless (as He promised, Rev. 1:3) the reading, study, and application of this vital portion of His Word to the glory of the Incomparable Christ.

Charles Lee Feinberg

INTRODUCTION

The name of the book. It is definitely not "The Revelation of St. John the Divine" (so AV). Better is "The Revelation of John." Best is "The Revelation of Jesus Christ" (cf. 1:1).

Authorship. The author of the book is John, the son of Zebedee, author of the Gospel of John and I, II, III John (cf. 1:1, 4, 9; 22:8). Donald Guthrie (*New Testament Introduction*, p. 933) has stated: ". . . There are few books in the New Testament with stronger early attestation." Apostolic authorship was questioned by Dionysius, Eusebius, the Council of Laodicea (c. A.D. 360), and the Peshitta Version (early fifth century).

Arguments for apostolic authorship are:

(1) *External evidence.* Those who witnessed to belief in apostolic authorship in the second and early third centuries were Justin, Irenaeus, Clement, Origen, Tertullian, and Hippolytus.

(2) *Internal evidence.*

a. He was known by the name John to the seven churches of Asia, and knew the activities of each church.

b. He writes with authority, expecting the churches to accept what he has written as a message from God.

c. His book, belonging to the style of apocalypse, is different from the non-canonical Jewish types. It is not attributed to an ancient worthy like Enoch or Baruch.

d. The writer is conscious of divine inspiration (1:1, 11, 19; 10:10; 22:6-8, 9, 18ff.).

e. Similarities of thought indicate a close relationship between the Apocalypse, the Gospel of John, and I, II, and III John. The affinities are seen in common ideas, theology, and wording. Cf. John 1:1 with Revelation 19:13; John 4:10 f., 14; 7:38 with Revelation 7:17; 21:6; 22:17; John 10:1ff. with Revelation 7:17; John 4:21 with Revelation 21:22. There is a marked use of antithesis in both books, e.g., the power of God and the power of the world; light and darkness; truth and falsehood.

Arguments against apostolic authorship (pro John the Elder) are:

(1) Linguistic differences. No one denies there are differences in language between the Revelation and the other works of John. Explanations have been given to account for these:

a. There was an interval of a score of years between the Gospel and the Revelation. But different grammatical constructions appear by choice.

b. Revelation differs from the Gospel because as prophecy it follows Old Testament patterns.

c. The use of amanuenses. There is no proof for this. Guthrie (*op. cit.* p. 942): "It should be noted, incidentally, that in spite of linguistic and grammatical differences the Apocalypse has a closer affinity to the Greek of the other Johannine books than to any other New Testament books."

(2) There are no apostolic claims. Since John's apostleship was not disputed (unlike Paul), there was no need to stress his office.

(3) Non-Johannine features. The doctrines of God, Christ, the Spirit, and future things are said to be dif-

ferent from the Gospel. Differences do not indicate incompatibility. There is progress in doctrine and necessary additions to doctrines already revealed.

(4) The conflicting traditions of the apostle's death, one at his old age at Ephesus and another earlier at the time of the martyrdom of James (Acts 12). The first is the stronger and more reliable tradition.

As to authorship by a John the Elder, there is no solid evidence that such a person ever lived. The view that the author was John the prophet is no more tenable than the position just given.

Place and date of writing. At Patmos where the Apostle John was exiled for the faith (1:9). Patmos, a small rocky island in the Mediterranean Sea, is about thirty-five miles southwest of Miletus. During the Roman Empire it was used as a place of banishment. Because of John's exile here the island was esteemed during subsequent times, although it was depopulated by pirates.

The date of the book is c. A.D. 95/96 in the reign of the Roman Emperor Domitian, which is the most generally accepted view. Most authorities feel the background of persecutions (1:9; 2:10. 13; 3:10; 6:9; 18:24) best fits the reign of Domitian (A.D. 51-96). The date in the reign of Nero (A.D. 37-68) has little to commend it.

Canonicity. A canonical book is one which carries divine authority and is normative for Christian belief and behavior. Revelation was early considered as part of the canon, but not all were persuaded. Justin, Melito of Sardis, Irenaeus, Tertullian, among others, accepted the book as the work of the Apostle John. On the other hand, the Eastern Church expressed doubts on the question and did not accord the Revelation canonicity until the fourth century. Luther, Zwingli, and Erasmus did not consider it apostolic; Calvin did not address the question. But in the light of uniform ancient tradition the book must be accorded canonical status (H.C. Thiessen, *Introduction to the New Testament,* pp. 318-319.)

Destination. The indicated destination of the book, as given in chapters 1, 2, and 3, was certain churches in Asia, specifically, Ephesus, Smyrna, Pergamum, Thyatira, Sardis, Philadelphia, and Laodicea. But unquestionably it was intended for other churches of that day and the church universal of all ages. The promise of blessing (1:3) cannot be restricted.

Place in the canon. It is in every sense of the word the capstone of the Bible, whose significance cannot be overestimated. It is indeed the grand consummation of all God's earthly and heavenly plans and the supreme vindication of Christ's Person and work.

Use of the Old Testament. The Apostle John, steeped in Old Testament truth, drew his concepts and symbols from Daniel, Ezekiel, Isaiah, and Zechariah, as well as Exodus, Jeremiah, and Joel (D. Guthrie, *op. cit.,* pp. 964-967). Although the apocalypse does not quote directly, its four hundred four verses contain about five-hundred fifty references to the Old Testament (B. F. Westcott and F. J. A. Hort, *Greek New Testament,* pp. 184 ff.).

Interpretation. There are four main interpretive approaches to the book:

(1) The Historical Method. This view claims the book covers the entire history of the church, as it pictures the antagonism of the forces of evil in the world against the church.

(2) The Praeterist. This approach sees the greater part of the prophecies as fulfilled in the past, especially in the

confrontation of the church with the Roman Empire. The victory of the church is foretold and assured.

(3) The Spiritual. This method of interpretation holds that the book manifests the ultimate and permanent triumph of truth over error.

(4) The Futurist Approach. This approach maintains that from chapter 4 all is predictive (1:3, 19).

Purpose of the book. The book exhibits a threefold purpose:

(1) It aimed to encourage believers in the times of the Roman persecutions of the early church by assuring them of the final victory of Christ.

(2) It enlarges upon and adds to Old Testament prophetic truth, especially in the area of the consummation of human history.

(3) It presents a vivid unveiling of the Lord Jesus Christ in His entrance upon His purchased possession throughout creation.

Style of the book. It is a message in symbolic language; 1:1: "signified," i.e., conveyed the message by signs. The book can only be properly understood in the light of scores of symbols and figures from the Old Testament.

Characteristics. The book is an "apocalypse," an unveiling or disclosure. This type of literature is found in Isaiah 24-27, 65, 66; Joel 2:1-11, 28-32; Zechariah 9-14; and especially in Daniel. There are certain general characteristics of apocalypse which distinguish this literature from prophecy in general. Prophecy and apocalyptic differ as to content. The predictive element in prophecy is more prominent in apocalyptic, covers longer periods of time, and is more comprehensive in its view of the world. Both prophecy and apocalypse tell of the coming of the Messiah, but in the latter it has a broader reference. In prophecy the rule of Messiah is mainly related to Israel; in apocalypse it is seen in relation to the dominant powers of the world (cf. Dan 7:13, 14; Rev 11:15). The prophet as a preacher of righteousness used prediction as a guarantee of his divine mission or as a display of the natural result of rebellion against God. The apocalyptist assigns great importance to prediction.

Prophecy and apocalyptic differ as to form. Prophecy uses visions, but they are implied rather than described. In apocalyptic the vision is the vehicle whereby the prediction is presented. In prophetic visions the symbols used are natural, e.g., the bones of Ezekiel 37. The visions of apocalyptic are arbitrary, e.g., the horns of the goat of Daniel 8. They have no basis in nature. Whereas the prophets wrote in a style that bordered on poetry, the apocalyptists always used prose.

Theme. The glorious theme of the book is the Lord Jesus Christ Himself as He enters upon His purchased possession. Specifically, He is revealed in representative chapters as follows:

Ch. 1 — The medium of God's revelation (vss. 1, 5)
Ch. 2 — The coming Ruler of the nations (v. 27)
Ch. 5 — The Lion of the tribe of Judah (v. 5)
        — The slain Lamb (v. 6)
Ch. 7 — The Lamb the Shepherd (v. 17)
Ch. 14 — The Lamb on Mt. Zion (v. 1)
Ch. 18 — The Judge of Babylon (v. 8)
Ch. 19— The Bridegroom (vss. 7-9)
        — King of Kings and Lord of Lords (v. 16)
Ch. 20 — The Reigning Christ (vss. 4-6)
Ch. 21 — The Alpha and the Omega (v. 6)
Ch. 22 — The Root and Offspring of David, the Morning Star (v. 16)

Critical questions. See under date and authorship.

Plan of the book (1:19)
(1) The things John saw. Ch. 1.
(2) The things which are. Chs. 2, 3.
(3) The things which shall occur after these things.
Chs. 4-22 (Dan 9:27).
a. Tribulation Period. Chs. 4-19.
b. Millennial Reign. Ch. 20.
c. Eternal glory. Chs. 21, 22.

OUTLINE OF THE BOOK

I. The Vision of the Risen Christ. Ch. 1.
A. The Introduction. 1:1-8.
1. Title of the book. 1:1.
2. Means of communication. 1:1, 2.
3. Blessing promised. 1:3.
4. Messages to the seven churches. 1:4-8.
a. Salutation from the Triune God. 1:4-6.
b. The visible return of Christ. 1:7.
c. The Author of the messages. 1:8.
B. The Vision on Patmos. 1:9-20.
1. The recipient of the vision. 1:9.
2. The place of the vision. 1:9.
3. The Revealer of the vision. 1:10.
4. The destination of the message. 1:11.
5. The content of the vision. 1:12-16.
a. The seven golden lampstands. 1:12.
b. The Son of Man. 1:13.
c. His head, hair, and eyes. 1:14.
d. His feet and voice. 1:15.
e. The seven stars; a sharp sword; His
face. 1:16.

5. Her name. 17:5.
6. Her bloodthirstiness. 17:6.
7. The mystery of the woman. 17:7.
8. Identity of the beast. 17:8-13.
9. The victory of the Lamb. 17:14-18.
B. Fall of Babylon. Ch. 18.
   1. The glorious angel. 18:1.
   2. Babylon's fall realized. 18:2.
   3. Babylon's guilt. 18:3.
   4. Call to flee the doomed city. 18:4-8.
   5. The mourning of kings and merchants. 18:9-20.
   6. The finality of her doom. 18:21-23.
   7. The reason for her fall. 18:24.
XIII. The Supper of the Lamb and the Supper of God. Ch. 19.
   A. Hallelujahs in Heaven. 19:1-6.
   B. The Marriage of the Lamb. 19:7-10.
   C. The Visible Coming of Christ. 19:11-16.
   D. The Supper of God: Armageddon. 19:17-19.
   E. Judgment of the Beast and False Prophet. 19:20, 21.
XIV. The Millennial Reign of Christ. Ch. 20.
   A. The Binding of Satan. 20:1-3.
   B. The Resurrection and Reign of the Saints. 20:4-6.
   C. The Final Doom of Satan, the Beast, and the False Prophet. 20:7-10.
   D. The Great White Throne Judgment. 20:11-15.
XV. The New Heaven and Earth. Ch. 21.
   A. Passing of Old Heaven and Earth. 21:1.
   B. New Jerusalem. 21:2-7.
   C. The Portion of the Ungodly. 21:8.
   D. The Wife of the Lamb. 21:9.
   E. Description of the New Jerusalem. 21:10-27.

3. Christ's coming with His rewards. 22:12.
4. His eternal character. 22:13.
5. The blessedness of the redeemed. 22:14.
6. The ungodly excluded. 22:15.
7. The Authenticator of the book. 22:16.
8. Invitation to the unsaved. 22:17.
9. Warnings against tampering with the prophecy. 22:18, 19.

M. The Testimony of Christ to His Coming. 22:20.

N. Benediction. 22:21.

1 The Vision of the Risen Christ

Chapter 1:1-20

A. The Introduction. 1:1-8.

1. Title of the book. 1:1.

The correct title for the book indicates that it is not a revelation of John, but of Jesus Christ. The unveiling treats of what He will accomplish in consummating time and ushering in eternity.

2. Means of communication. 1:1, 2.

1, 2. So significant is the truth embodied in the message of the book that there is a fivefold avenue of transmission of the word: the Father to the Son to the mediating angel to John the apostle/prophet to God's servants. Emphasis is laid on the fact that John not only heard messages, but he saw visions as well (Gr *osa eiden*).

Things which must shortly take place. This statement gives no basis for the historical interpretation of the book. Events are here seen from the perspective of the Lord and not from the human viewpoint (cf. II Pet 3:8). The same Greek words appear in Luke 18:7, 8 (Gr *en tachei*), where the delay is clearly a prolonged one.

He sent and communicated it by His angel. He signified (Gr *esēmanen*) the message, that is, He conveyed it by signs to the angel. In both the Old and New Testament the ministry of angels is employed with regard to future events (Ezk 1:5 ff.; Dan 8:16; Zech 1:9; Acts 8:26; 10:3, 7).

3. The promised blessing. 1:3.

Only this book in the Bible pronounces a blessing on the one who reads (singular because with few copies of the Scriptures in those days, one read while many could hear), those who hear and heed (obey) the things written in it. Scripture can only be effective when applied in the life. It is vital to notice that the book is called "the prophecy." Future things are at the heart of the book.

The time is near. The words (Gr *o kairos engus*) appear only twice in the Revelation. Neither reference indicates the possible length involved. Again, all is seen from the perspective of God.

4. Messages to the seven churches. 1:4-8.

a. Salutation from the Triune God. 1:4-6.

4. John to the seven churches that are in Asia. The writer is the Apostle John (see Introduction), who is mentioned besides here in 1:1, 9; 22:8. Asia does not refer to the continent of Asia, but rather to the Roman province of Asia Minor. There were other churches in the province (e.g., Colosse), but these where chosen because of specific characteristics in them. The salutation combines both the Greek (grace) and Hebrew (peace) elements found in the New Testament books, and issues from all the Godhead: the sevenfold fullness of the Holy Spirit (cf. Isa 11:2), the eternal Father, and Jesus Christ the Mediator.

5. Christ is seen in His threefold office as prophet, priest, and king. The Father is on the throne; the Spirit is before the throne; and the Son is connected with the earth as supreme ruler. The doxology is carried through from this verse to the next. It is directed to Christ in His ever-present love (*loved us*) and accomplished release of His own from sin by the work of Calvary.

6. As redeemed ones believers constitute a kingdom and are priests before God. Since Christ is both king and priest, His own partake of His nature and offices. Notice the emphasis on kingdom and dominion, a dual objective

of the entire book (cf. Rev 20:6; also II Tim 2:12).
   b. The visible return of Christ. 1:7.
   7. The second coming of Christ to earth in fulfillment
of Old Testament prediction (cf. Dan 7:13) will be seen by
all living on earth at the time, Israel and the nations. The
time is that spoken of in Zechariah 12:10. But believers
also now long for that coming.
   c. The Author of the messages. 1:8.
   8. The Three Persons of the Trinity put their
authoritative seal to the message.
   B. The Vision on Patmos. 1:9-20.
   1. The recipient of the vision. 1:9.
   9. John, already seen in verse 4, identifies himself
with his readers as a brother and partaker with them of
the tribulation, kingdom, and perseverance of Jesus. The
tribulation referred to is not that so fully described in the
Revelation, but those trials common to all believers in
this life (cf. Acts 14:22), and more particularly endured in
that day under the widespread persecutions of Domitian
the Roman Emperor. The kingdom mentioned may indicate that of verse 6 or more probably that kingdom on
earth to be established through the coming of the Lord
Jesus to earth. The perseverance spoken of is that patience and steadfastness required in the midst of persecutions.
   2. The place of the vision. 1:9.
   9. Indeed, John was that hour writing from a lonely
island where he had been banished for his fidelity to the
Word of God.
   3. The Revealer of the vision. 1:10.
   10. Just as all Scripture is given by the inspiration of
the Spirit, so John was under the control of the Spirit
when the vision was revealed to him. What is meant by
"the Lord's Day"? J. A. Seiss (*The Apocalypse*, pp. 17-19),
among others, considered the phrase could mean only the

Day of the Lord referred to so many times in the Old
Testament and elaborated on in the Revelation. However,
the majority of expositors are surely correct in
understanding the reference to be to the first day of the
week, Sunday. A.T. Robertson (*Word Pictures in the
New Testament*, Vol. VI, p. 290) has written: "Deissmann
has proven (*Bible Studies*, p. 217 f.; *Light*, etc., p. 357 ff.)
from inscriptions and papyri that the word *kuriakos* was
in common use for the sense 'imperial' . . . and from papyri
and ostraca that *hēmera Sebastē* (Augustus Day) was the
first day of each month . . . It was easy, therefore, for the
Christians to take this term, already in use, and apply it
to the first day of the week in honour of the Lord Jesus
Christ's resurrection on that day . . . In the N.T. the word
occurs only here and I Cor. 11:20 (*kuriakon deipnon* the
Lord's Supper). It has no reference to *hēmera kuriou* (the
day of judgment, II Pet. 3:10)."

The loud voice is that of Christ (vs. 15) and is likened to
a trumpet sound to indicate that the message was a matter of great public importance.

4. The destination of the message. 1:11.

11. The seven churches (vs. 4) to whom the book is
sent, are named in the order messengers would carry letters, going from northwest to northeast and southeast.

5. The content of the vision. 1:12-16.

a. The seven golden lampstands. 1:12.

12. There is an allusion to the lampstands in the
tabernacle and temple, the difference being they were all
united there, whereas they are separate here with Christ
in the midst in the place of preeminent authority. The
churches are seen in their sphere of earthly authority.

b. The Son of man. 1:13.

13. Christ is revealed as High Priest coming in judgment, yet as the serving One (the golden girdle).

c. His head, hair, and eyes. 1:14.

14. The description of the Lord Jesus Christ is reminiscent of the judgment scene of Daniel 7:13, 14. What is stated in Daniel of the Ancient of Days (the Father) is true of the Son, because they are both truly divine.

d. His feet and voice. 1:15.

15. In judgment Christ will trample the winepress of God's wrath (Isa 63:1-5). His powerful voice will not be lifted to quiet the troubled sea, but to call down the judgment of God on the wicked.

e. The seven stars, a sword, and His face. 1:16.

16. The seven stars (to be explained in vs. 20) are under His complete control with security. The sword is His Word (cf. Heb 4:12; Rev 19:15, 21), which will be active in the coming judgments. As for His blessed face, here are brilliance, splendor, and holy strength.

6. John's reaction. 1:17a.

17. Though John had fellowshipped with the Lord in His earthly ministry, the vision of the risen Christ was so glorious and overpowering that John fell as a dead man.

7. Assurance for John. 1:17b, 18.

17b, 18. John is reassured by Christ's word concerning His Person and nature. He is the eternal One; He dominates time: He lived, lives, and lives forever. He has supreme authority over death (the body) and Hades (the soul).

8. The command to write. 1:19.

19. This is the key verse of the book; it indicates the threefold plan of the prophecy (see Introduction); and it is the only safe guide to its correct interpretation.

9. Interpretation of the seven stars and seven lampstands. 1:20.

20. The angels are not literal angels, nor believers in general, but, as chapters 2 and 3 show, are pastors or ministers of the local churches in places of authority and

responsibility. Local congregations are likened to lampstands in order to convey their function of testimony and spread of the light of the gospel.

2 The Letters To The Seven Churches

Chapters 2 and 3

A. The Letter to the Church of Ephesus. 2:1-7.

There are seven churches chosen, because in Scripture seven is the number of completion. In these seven letters the Spirit gives a complete picture of the moral and spiritual history of the church, along with other truths. The letters have seven exhortations to hear them, yet they are sadly neglected. The messages have spiritual, historical, and prophetic value. Since chapter 1 dealt with the things John saw — the risen Christ — and chapters 2 and 3 treat of the things that are, then they are pertinent to the church age from Pentecost to the Rapture. Each letter has four elements: (1) the manner in which Christ presents Himself; (2) the commendation (or condemnation) He gives; (3) the reward He promises; and (4) the exhortation to hear. The messages refer to distinct, historical churches in the province of Asia, hence timely; they also apply to types of believers in every age, hence timeless. Ephesus may be characterized as the church of departed love.

1. The description of Christ. 2:1.

1. In the history of the church this congregation speaks of the apostolic period. Ephesus was the main center of Grecian culture and heathen idolatry. Here was located the temple of the goddess Artemis (Diana), adorned and ornamented by all of Asia, one of the seven

wonders of the ancient world (cf. Acts 19). Aquila, Priscilla, and Apollos labored in this city, and Paul preached here for three years at one time. In Ephesus John, having left his home in Jerusalem, ministered for thirty years.

Christ is seen here in the proper place as guiding, controlling, and ruling over all. His servants are secure, since He holds them firmly in His right hand. Outwardly, everything is in proper order.

2. Commendation of the church. 2:2, 3, 6.

2, 3. In each letter it is indicated that Christ has absolute knowledge of what transpires in each local congregation. Deeds, toil, and perseverance are all virtues. Moreover, the Ephesians put to the test those claiming apostolic authority. The apostles were dying, and perhaps John was the only one left. The Ephesians kept their doctrine pure.

6. Further commendation is stated, because the Ephesians hated the deeds of the Nicolaitans, lit., "conquerors of the people." It is not known who they were, although some interpreters try to connect them with some sect. Archbishop Richard C. Trench states simply, "Nicolaitanism is clerisy" (*Lectures on the Book of Revelation*, p. 52).

3. Rebuke of the church. 2:4, 5.

4. In spite of all the commendable qualities of this church, there was one vital lack: they had left their first love. This was true of the church whose name means "desired." Their hearts were drifting away from Christ. The first love is marked by its all-engrossing quality, its fervency, and constancy. It can be seen in the words of Philippians 1:21. The first danger sign for any believer is to grow cold toward Christ. A church may have great zeal and activity, soundness of doctrine and practice, yet have its first love for Christ on the decline. It is subtle. Love

looks for love and meticulous care with doctrine and discipline will not take its place. Loss of first love can be so easily followed by evils in doctrine and practice. Christ will have all the believer's love or none (cf. Lk 10:38-42). 5. The church is commanded to repent or suffer removal. This does not mean individuals lose their salvation, but the church can forfeit its place of light bearing and witness. Ephesus is a city now wrapped in the mantle of Islam. The light of the church has indeed been moved. 4. The command to hear. 2:7a.

7a. It is clear that the message and warning of this church were for all in that day, but the admonition is pertinent to all believers today. 5. The promise to the overcomer. 2:7b.

7b. The Paradise of God expresses the blessedness of heaven. Possibly, Ephesus had tried to make her Paradise here on earth, so allowed her love to grow cold. Cf. Colossians 3:1, 2.

B. The Letter to the Church of Smyrna. 2:8-11.
   1. The description of Christ. 2:8.

8. The letter to Smyrna is the shortest of the letters; that to Thyatira is the longest. Smyrna was originally an Ionian settlement which passed into decline in process of time. Rebuilt by Alexander the Great and Antigonue, it became immediately wealthy and famous. It was about forty miles north of Ephesus. In some respects it was the rival of Ephesus in olden days. Because of its natural and commercial situation, its wealth, commerce, and splendid buildings, it was called "the beautiful." It was not far behind Ephesus in idolatry. This city is not named in the Acts or the epistles of Paul, so it is not known when the gospel came there. The Roman imperial laws against Christianity were strenuously enforced in Smyrna. The persecutions of believers in Asia Minor were centered here. Polycarp, friend of John and the last disciple who

knew the apostle personally, is said to have been slain here in A.D. 168. It is generally believed that Polycarp was "the angel of the church in Smyrna."

Christ's eternal nature and deity are expressed in absolute terms. The infinite Saviour is supreme before all things and all time. He is also the last as the goal of all things (cf. Rom 11:36). His great triumph over death is next stated. He has destroyed death and its power. How important that Christ should be revealed in this light to the suffering and persecuted church. It was the period of the Roman persecutions of the church which lasted for two centuries. Smyrna means "myrrh," which must be crushed to give forth its fragrance. In the martyr age the church yielded a sweet fragrance to God (cf. II Cor 2:14-16).

2. Commendation of the church. 2:9.

9. The Lord informs them that He knows their tribulation (Gr *thlipsis*), a word that conveys the idea of pressing grapes until the juice comes forth. Christ has gone to the utmost depths of suffering and death. He sometimes permits trials in order to rekindle lost first love (Ps 119:67). Furthermore, He knows their poverty (cf. II Cor 8:9); they had, like Hebrew believers of a former time (Heb 10:34), suffered the loss of everything. Confiscation of goods attended and followed persecution. But they are reminded that though poor in worldly goods, they were rich in faith (cf. 1 Cor 3:21-23). The risen Christ informs them that He knows the reviling of the synagogue of Satan. The reference is not to the Jewish nation in general. What is meant is the legalizing, Judaizing movement of the early Christian era. It was Galatianism which made its appearance in the apostolic and sub-apostlic age, because men tried to dilute the grace of God with legalism and ceremonialism. Satan's synagogue is here in opposition to the church of God. Satan attacked

this church from without by persecution and from within by perversion of doctrine. The evil had evidently not made inroads into this church, for there is no censure or command to repent.

3. The coming trial and call to faithfulness. 2:10.

10. It is interesting that there is no word that the Smyrnans would escape their suffering. But even more, they are told their trials would be increased. They were tortured, exposed to wild bulls and lions that tore them to pieces. In the Roman Empire imprisonment was not a form of punishment as today, because the government was not willing to support a multitude of prisoners. A man in prison was either awaiting his trial or death. As for the ten days, there were ten persecutions from Nero to Diocletian (A.D. 312). They were under Nero, Domitian, Trajan, Antoninus, Severus, Maximian, Decius, Valerian, Aurelian, and Diocletian. Too, Diocletian's persecution lasted ten years.

They are encouraged to be faithful until death, not just as long as they lived, but even if it cost them their lives. The call speaks not of extensiveness but of intensity. In the Old Testament saints were delivered from death (cf. Job 2:6; Dan 3:19-30; 6:16-24), but in the New they triumph over death. Their hope was to be dependent on the Lord. The reward was to be the crown of life. Christ Himself, faithful until death, was crowned with life on resurrection morning. Believers may be rewarded with one or more of five crowns (2:10; 4:4; II Tim 4:8; Jas 1:12; I Pet 5:4).

4. The command to hear. 2:11a.

5. The promise to the overcomer. 2:11b.

11b. The second death is eternal death (cf. 20:6, 14; 21:8). It is the portion of all the unsaved. Notice how well this promise is suited to those who were threatened with the first death.

C. The Letter to the Church of Pergamum. 2:12-17.

1. The description of Christ. 2:12.

12. Pergamum lay north of Smyrna and was considered one of the finest cities of Asia. It had little or no commerce, but was remarkable for its learning, refinement, and science, especially medicine. A number of kings made this their royal residence. Its famous library, second only to that of Alexandria, consisted of 200,000 books. Ephesus and Smyrna were evil cities, but Pergamum was especially so in its idolatry. Here was to be found the renowned temple of Aesculapius in which the most prominent object was the wreathed serpent. The early science of medicine was identified with the worship of Satan who usurped the place and dignity of Christ, for they called Aesculapius, the "Preserver" and "Saviour."

As Ephesus was the church of departed love, and Smyrna the church of fiery persecutions, so Pergamum (meaning marriage) was the church of worldly alliance. This was the period in the history of the church when she was elevated to a place of power and married to the world. It was the era when church and state came together under the reign of Constantine (A.D. 313) and his successors. After the reign of Diocletian, there was a power struggle between Constantine and Maxentius, with victory going to the former, who claimed he had a vision of a cross with these words (in Latin): "In this sign conquer." Upon his accession to the throne of Rome, Constantine declared Christianity the official religion.

Christ is revealed as the One holding the sharp two-edged sword. This is undoubtedly the Word of God. Cf. John 5:22, 27; Hebrews 4:12. Since this church is tolerating error, it needs to have the measuring rule of God's Word brought into action.

2. Commendation of the church. 2:13.

13. Satan's throne speaks of his usurped world power. He is identified in Scripture as the prince of this

world (cf. Mt 4:8, 9; II Cor 4:4). In the Smyrna age Satan tried to destroy the church by persecution. In the next centuries he tried to ruin her testimony by patronage without and false principles within. Constantine's attitude toward the church brought many into it who were pagan at heart. Gibbon, in his famous work on the decline and fall of the empire, stated: "The salvation of the common people was purchased at an easy rate, if it be true that in one year 12,000 men were baptized at Rome, besides a proportionable number of women and children, and that a white garment with twenty pieces of gold had been promised by the emperor to every convert." In many cases heathen were won over by adoption of pagan rites and festivals as parts of Christian worship. The union of church and state has wrought havoc wherever introduced, as attested in ancient times and to this day.

"Hold fast My name" may well refer to the Arian controversy, which lasted for over a century and was finally settled in A.D. 325 by the Council of Nicaea (S.E. France on the Mediterranean Sea). They did not deny Christ's name, for the essential deity of the Lord Jesus Christ was maintained. The commendation of Antipas (literally, "Against all"), the martyr, is explicit indeed. He is unknown to us, but God knows all His faithful witnesses.

3. Rebuke of the church. 2:14, 15.

14. In Ephesus there was one cause of censure; here Christ says "a few things." Pergamum was one of the fulfillments of Paul's warning in Acts 20:29, 30. Notice the decline from Ephesus where the deeds of the Nicolaitans were hated, to Pergamum where their teaching was held and tolerated. It appears that the teaching of Balaam and that of the Nicolaitans are distinct, but they have the same disastrous results. Numbers 25:1-9 gives a clear picture of the union of church and state. Balaam taught Balak how to draw Israel away from their position of

separation (Num 23:9).

15. The teaching of the Nicolaitans, as already noticed in the church of Ephesus, has reference to clericalism,
which developed rapidly in this era of the church. There
is no basis in Scripture now for a special class of priests,
such as God instituted in Israel (cf. Lev 8). The ultimate
claim of Nicolaitanism is infallibility.

4. Call to repentance. 2:16.

16. The church was called upon to exercise its
discipline. The coming mentioned is a judicial visitation in
speedy judgment according to the Word of God.

5. The command to hear. 2:17a.

6. The promise to the overcomer. 2:17b.

17b. Manna (literally, "What is it?") in the Old Testament was not hidden. For 12,500 mornings the Lord rain-
ed this bread from heaven for His people. It was later
preserved (cf. Ex 16:33; Heb 9:4). Notice the contrast between the hidden manna (type of Christ, Jn 6) and the
public glory of union with the world. To go to the place of
separation with Christ, the hidden manna, is greater gain
than consorting with the world. The white stone speaks
of the custom of casting such a stone into a voter's urn
with the name of a candidate, indicating the approval of
the one who cast it. Special divine approval will be the
portion of the godly nucleus in Pergamum.

D. The Letter to the Church of Thyatira. 2:18-29.

1. The description of Christ. 2:18.

18. Thyatira lay southeast of Pergamum. Ephesus,
Smyrna, and Pergamum were more noted than Thyatira,
which, nevertheless, has an interest of its own. The city is
first mentioned in connection with Paul's missionary
labors in Europe. His first convert on that continent was
a woman of Thyatira, Lydia, a seller of purple, a commodity for which the city was famous (cf. Acts 16:14). The city

was founded by Seleucid I, the first of the Seleucid dynasty (early fourth century A.D.), although it had been inhabited before that time, and indeed when John wrote. It came to be a garrison city and military post because of its unfavorable natural condition — an open valley with great sloping hills of moderate elevation — which had to be strengthened in the interest of security. It is the longest of all the letters. It marks the beginning of the second group of letters in which the moral history goes on to the second coming of Christ. In this and the following letters the call to hear comes after the promise. The title "The Son of God" is used only here in the Revelation.

Thyatira, which means "continual sacrifice," is the church of clerical domination. It designates the period in the history of the church from the sixth or seventh century to the Reformation in the sixteenth century. The dominant church of that period promoted continual sacrifice in its service.

18. When anyone is permitted to usurp the place of Christ, the emphasis must be placed on Him as Son of God, rather than the son of Mary. The title is meant to convey power and authority. The Saviour is revealed as searching, penetrating, and judging. His eyes discern evil, for He cannot tolerate it. His feet of bronze indicate that He stamps out evil with judgment (cf. as a parallel Isa 63:1-6).

2. Commendation of the church. 2:19.

19. This church has much evil in it, but Christ looks first at what can be commended. These are the strongest words of commendation addressed to any of the churches. There were devotion and zeal in the Middle Ages in spite of the apostasy and corruption of the majority. The later works were more than the first, because the darker the night the more ardent were the company of the godly minority.

3. Rebuke of the church. 2:20, 21.

20. The woman of Jezebel (cf. I Kgs 19-21) was the wife of Ahab and the source of idolatry in Israel. Balaam attacked Israel from without; she, from within. Recall that she was a stranger in Israel; she was responsible for the worst idolatry in the nation; and she persecuted the servants of God. She calls herself (never called of God) a prophetess, claiming infallibility in setting forth doctrine and new revelation from God. The dogmas of papal Rome are clearly discerned. This church leads astray by her teaching; it is away from divine authority to man's. But there is still a remnant of the faithful bondservants of Christ. As a counterpart of Jezebel of old, there is a godless consorting with the world and an intricate system of worship of idols.

21. In His grace and forbearance God gave this church time to repent. Godly men called upon the church to repent, but she refused to do so. Therefore, there is no call to repent in this letter. Only judgment remains. This church remains apart from the truth of God until she is joined with all the systems of religious evil of the world (cf. Rev 18, 19).

4. Warning to the church. 2:22, 23.

22. In this portion there are three groups: Jezebel, those who dabble with her system perhaps from a spirit of tolerance or unity, and her children, i.e., her adherents. Notice that her judgment is in the very place of her corruption.

23. The lesson given is both individual (to Thyatira) and general (to all the churches).

5. Counsel to the godly. 2:24, 25.

24. The rest who are in Thyatira are evidently a godly remnant who did not follow the corruptions of the church, but rather denounced its unbiblical ways. The Lord in compassion would lay no other burden on them;

they were suffering much for the truth.

25. Since there is no hope that the corrupt church will repent, the godly in her can only in faithful holding to the truth look for the coming of the Lord. The fact that the Thyatira saints are seen to go on to the time of Christ's coming reveals that the church as such goes on beyond its original period in the Middle Ages.

6. Promise to the overcomer. 2:26-28.

26. Those who refuse the advantages of the world, which the ungodly prematurely enjoy, will yet enter into the ample privileges provided for them by Christ (cf. II Tim 2:12). Theirs will be a blessed portion in the coming kingdom of Christ on earth.

27. Since this is not usurped authority, it will be enjoyed and will endure (cf. Ps 2:7-9). Mark you, the authority granted the faithful will come from God the Father, as did Christ's.

28. The morning star (cf. II Pet 1:19; Rev 22:16) is the promise of being with Christ before the day breaks; it is the promise of the Rapture. Israel awaits the Sun of righteousness (cf. Mal 4:20); the church looks for the Morning Star (cf. 22:16).

7. The command to hear. 2:29.

29. The message to this church, as all the rest, has an application to all believers at all times.

E. The Letter to the Church of Sardis. 3:1-6.

1. The description of Christ. 3:1.

Sardis is about twenty-seven miles due south of Thyatira. It was one of the oldest and greatest cities of Western Asia. In ancient times it was a proud, wealthy city, and the capital of the kingdom of Lydia. It had a history of many wars, and was the city of the wealthy Croesus. The patron deity of the city was Cybele, whose form appeared on their coins. She was represented as half-human and was regularly associated with a pair of lions or single lion. The deity was supposed to have power to restore the dead. The city fell before Cyrus the Great of Persia in the sixth century B.C. In A.D. 17 the city suffered greatly from an earthquake. When John wrote this letter, the city was a city of the past. Later it was restored and continued to flourish until A.D. 1400-1403, when the Tartar Tamerlane swept over the area and destroyed everything. The city has never recovered from this desolation.

Sardis (probably meaning "remnant") was the church of empty profession. This period in the history of the church was that of the Reformation. The moral and spiritual corruption of the church of the Middle Ages, together with the evangelical preaching of certain godly leaders, brought about needed reform.

1. Paul speaks of the unity of the Person of the Spirit (cf. Eph 4:3); John emphasizes the diversity of His attributes and actions as well as the fullness of His power (cf. Isa 11:2). In the different creeds of Christendom, it will be remembered, the Holy Spirit was not given His rightful place. The seven stars are an allusion to the way Christ was revealed to the Church of Ephesus. The Reformation itself was God's work; the resulting ecclesiastical systems were of man. Man is ever prone to error, so the results of the period reveal the presence of error and shortcoming. Sadly, the Lord commends nothing in this church. The measure of its privilege and profession was the measure of its responsibility. It was full of empty profession, hence dead. Again, the union of church and state brought about more profession than life.

2. Call to repentance. 3:2, 3.

2. The call to be watchful and wakeful was directed to the spiritual leaders to carry out their responsibility. They were exhorted to strengthen the remaining things,

because they had the testimony of the Word of God more fully than they who were engulfed in ecclesiastical formalism of the former period. It may surprise many to learn that not all truth was recovered in the Reformation, but this verse indicates that all was not complete in the sight of God. It was not a complete return to the apostolic church. Areas of doctrine and behavior were left incomplete, i.e., truths of Ephesians and Colossians were not emphasized by the reformers. How much of the truth of the Holy Spirit was there? of life truth? of prophetic truth?

3. Sardis believers are alerted to recall how much of recovered truth they had, and to keep the good they had received. Also, they needed to repent of the inadequate use they were making of it. If the church did not awake, they were in danger of meeting Christ when they were not ready. Mark you, the Lord does not come to believers as a thief, but to professors only.

3. Reward for the worthy. 3:4.

4. In spite of all appearances there was a godly remnant in this church. They had not defiled and soiled their garments (cf. Jas 1:27). The worthiness spoken of is a reckoning of grace; they had been made such by Christ.

4. Promise to the overcomer. 3:5.

5. There are actually three promised here. Garments are only made white in the blood of the Lamb (cf. 7:14). The promise not to erase the name from the book of life is strong assurance of the eternal security of the believer in Sardis. Moreover, Christ will delight to recognize as His own all overcomers. The method of overcoming is clear throughout the Word (cf. I Jn 5:4).

5. The command to hear. 3:6.

6. This is a simple call to a simple act, but so seldom heeded.

F. The Letter to the Church of Philadelphia. 3:7-13.
   1. The description of Christ. 3:7.
      7. The city was named after its founder Attalus
Philadelphus, king of Pergamum (159-138 B.C.), because
he was loyal to his brother Eumenes. It was situated
twenty-five miles south of Sardis. Its modern name is
Allah Shehr ("city of God"). The remains of early Christian times are more numerous here than in any other of
the cities named by John. It was a missionary city in the
Greek world in promoting unity of spirit, customs, and
loyalty within the kingdom (cf. W. M. Ramsay, *The Letters to the Seven Churches*, pp. 391-412). It is the only one
of the seven churches whose name has been preserved to
this day in the city founded by William Penn. This church
is the church of the faithful remnant. The reference appears to be to no distinct church period. There are no
words of censure for them. Philadelphia ("brotherly
love") may cover the times of revivals and missions which
began in the eighteenth and nineteenth centuries after
the deadening effect of doctrinal controversies and state-
church union in the midst of professing Protestantism.
The letter is manifestly to faithful individuals in all
groups of professing Christians.
      The One speaking is holy in life and true in doctrine,
holy in character and true in action. Christ is not revealed
in this character in chapter 1. He is seen here not in His
judicial nature, but in His personal character and attributes. The key of David is mentioned in connection
with the treasurer of David's house in Isaiah 22:22. He
opens by His Spirit the truths of the Word and no man
can shut; to hardened spirits He shuts and none can open.
Christ is also the key to the Word of God. Here is revealed His administrative authority as well; He opens and
shuts doors of ministry (cf. Acts 16:6-10). Connected with
David, He is depicted in His Messianic, kingly office.

2. Commendation of the church. 3:8.

8. The open door is that of witness and testimony including the worldwide mission field. To be sure, it is not a matter of human power and ingenuity, for these believers had little power. But no individual or group has power to frustrate the service of those joined to Christ. Their weakness is their defense (cf. II Cor 12:10). Smyrna and Philadelphia are the only churches without reproof; the one is a suffering church, the other, a weak one. Moreover, this church kept Christ's Word, speaking of their obedience and submission (cf. Jn 14:23). Nor have they denied the name of Christ: obedience and no apostasy.

3. Reward for faithfulness. 3:9, 10.

9. Since there is a return to first principles in this assembly, Satan again marshals his old attacks. He injects legalism; it is the Judaizing system in its opposition to the truth of grace. This is not true Old Testament theology.

10. Because they have persevered in the Word, the promise is that they will be kept from (not through) the hour of testing, which is the Tribulation Period (chs. 6-19), that is to come on the whole world of those who have completely settled down on earth (Gk is not merely oikeō, to dwell, but katoikeō, to settle down, which is contrary to the pilgrim nature of the church, cf. Phil 3:18-20; I Pet 2:11).

4. Exhortation to steadfastness. 3:11.

11. Because Christ will come suddenly, they were not to surrender one iota of Christ's word that they possessed then. If the truth is relinquished, the crown is lost. Notice the word is not that anyone would take their salvation, but their crown. A faithless servant may lose his crown, but not eternal life. Lost opportunities will result in lost crowns.

5. Promise to the overcomer. 3:12.

12. Notice the repetition of "My God." The promises are full of identification and appropriation. The pillar reminds of the two in the temple of Solomon (cf. I Kgs 7:21) and connote stability, strength, and permanence. Those who have been with Christ in the day of His rejection will realize the glory of the day of His enthronement.

6. The command to hear. 3:13.

13. A command to believers to hear is never out of place, because it is a long spiritual exercise to be quick to hear.

G. The Letter to the Church of Laodicea. 3:14-22.

1. The description of Christ. 3:14

Laodicea is about forty miles southeast of Philadelphia. Built by the Seleucid monarch, Antiochus II (261-246 B.C.), it was named after his wife, Laodice. It was a city of considerable size, trade, and wealth, specializing in the manufacture of wool. It was the bone of contention in Asia Minor under the Romans and under the Turks. In later times it was a Christian city of importance and the residence of a bishop, as well as the meeting place of church councils. Pride and self-satisfaction characterized the people and made their impress on the church as well. The city was destroyed by the Moslems in the Middle Ages, and the site of the once wealthy city is a mass of ruins.

14. Laodicea (meaning "rights of the people") is the church of insipid lukewarmness. It describes the moral condition of the church at the close of the church age. The people demand their rights with the result of democracy and almost anarchy (cf. II Tim 4:3). There is nothing to commend in this church although it thinks it is perfect (cf. vs. 17). Christ refers to Himself as The Amen, the One who establishes all God's promises. He is the Last Word,

the Ultimate Authority, the Finality of all things. When the church in her closing days will be unfaithful and untrue, He is seen as the Faithful and true Witness (cf. 1:5). All God's witnesses in time have failed at one time or other, but Christ never. Moreover, He is the Beginning of the creation of God. This does not invalidate His eternality. It indicates that He is Head of the new creation (cf. II Cor. 5:17).

2. Rebuke of the church. 3:15-17.

15. The fault with this church is that it is neither cold nor hot; there is neither zeal for God nor absolute repudiation of the Lord. Lukewarmness (lukewarm water is an emetic) is hot and cold together: in Laodicea there are great humanitarian and cultural projects without the saving grace of the gospel. Here is the attitude of the professing group toward Christ; they are totally indifferent. It is worse to be lukewarm (evangelical but not evangelistic, as many say) than to be one who abandons all profession. An active, positive position (notice Paul on the Damascus road) could be dealt with better.

16. Spitting the church out of Christ's mouth has no reference to loss of salvation, but removal from a place of witness. When believers are raptured, the Laodicean Church will remain on earth, spewed out by Christ to endure the Tribulation Period.

17. This church claims it has need of nothing, self-satisfied and self-complacent. Boasting of wealth and methods and organization, it fails to realize its absence of spiritual life. Christ informs them they are utterly insensitive to their condition.

3. Counsel for the church. 3:18.

18. For their threefold need (poverty, nakedness, and blindness) they are advised to buy, without money and price to be sure (cf. Isa 55:1), gold, which speaks of divine righteousness, white garments, which denote practical

righteousness, and eye salve, which points to spiritual discernment. Their trouble was that they had never really seen themselves as sinners.

4. Call to repentance. 3:19.

19. The reason for the rebuke and counsel was His love. If not for this, He would have forsaken her before this. The mass will not heed, but individuals do (so the singular Gk verbs). Grace is still open to individuals.

5. Invitation to accept Christ. 3:20.

20. Here is a tragic picture, but a true one: a group professing the name of Christ, but keeping Him on the outside. He is knocking at the door of the church for an individual to let Him in ("dine with him"). Christ may disown the church as a whole, but He still makes His plea to the individual heart.

6. Promise to the overcomer. 3:21.

21. To sit with Christ on His throne is indicative of royal authority, power, and glory. Kingdom participation is here in view. Christ will have His throne (cf. II Sam 7:13; Lk 1:31-33; Mt 25:31). He is now on the Father's throne (cf. Ps 110:1; Heb 1:3; 8:1; 10:12, 13; 12:2). The overcomer will reign with the victorious Christ on His blessed glorious throne.

7. The command to hear. 3:22.

22. The tireless Spirit of God still pleads with the individual heart.

3 The Vision of the Throne in Heaven

Chapters 4 and 5

A. The Creator on the Throne. 4:1-11.

    1. The call to ascend. 4:1.

Thus far in the book there have been covered the first two divisions of the prophecy (cf. 1:19): the things John saw (ch. 1) and the things which are during the church age (chs. 2, 3). The largest section of the book (chs. 4-22) is divisible into three parts (chs. 4-19; ch. 20; chs. 21, 22), all relating the things that are to be "after these things," subsequent to the church period. The same words (Gr *meta tauta*) appear in 1:19 and 4:1 (twice). Chapters 4 through 19 cover the seventieth week of Daniel (cf. Dan 9:27), known as the Tribulation Period. Recall that all this is to be fulfilled in the future after the church is taken home to heaven, if the consistent chronology of the Revelation is to be adhered to. It is clear how many times the word "church" has appeared in the first three chapters; it does not occur again until 22:16. The bride of chapter 19 is the church, but no other references occur with that word during the time of trial on earth.

    1. John is commanded to come up to heaven, so that he may see and understand from that vantage point the things that are to transpire on earth. Christ Himself has changed His position: in chapters 1-3 He was seen among the lampstands on earth; now He is in heaven. A number of expositors see the call to John as that of I Thessalo-

nians 4:16, 17; namely, the Rapture of the church. H. A.
Ironside has put it concisely: "Of this the rapture of the
apostle is the symbol" (*Lectures on the Revelation*, p. 80),
a view held by many others. It is the position of this commentary that the Rapture does occur after chapter 3, but
there are more compelling reasons than the one just
stated, as will be shown below.

2. The throne and its Occupant. 4:2, 3.

2. The throne in heaven occupies the attention of
John first, as it will the adoration of the redeemed. The
throne is occupied by the Son (cf. Jn 5:22), though neither
the Father nor the Spirit is excluded.

3. When heavenly things are spoken of, the description beggars earthly speech, so beautiful and durable
precious stones are introduced (cf. ch. 21). Jasper is of
various brilliant colors, and sardius is a red color. These
stones were the first and last precious stones in the
breastplate of the high priest. Cf. Exodus 28:17-20.
Emerald is green. The rainbow reveals God in covenant
relation with nature (cf. Gen 9:16). He does not forget His
promises. Many judgments in this book will be poured out
on the earth, but it is not the purpose of God to bring
about earth's utter destruction.

3. The twenty-four elders and thrones. 4:4.

4. As important as 3:10 is for the pretribulation Rapture, so is this crucial verse. In fact, it is decisive in the
matter. How so when it only speaks of twenty-four elders
and twenty-four thrones? The reasons are these: (a) the
elders are enthroned. Cf. 3:21. (b) Their number is important. The Levitical priesthood had twenty-four courses
(shifts) in Israel (cf. I Chr 24:7-19). The church is a
priesthood (cf. I Pet 2:5-9; Rev 1:6). (c) Their office is indicative; it is an eldership, a representative office, show-
ing they are not to be understood in an individual capacity. Cf. Acts 15:2; 20:17. (d) Their testimony is distinctive

(cf. 5:9, 10). This is true only of the church. (e) They display spiritual insight and are acquainted with the counsels of God (5:5; 7:13; Jn 15:15). (f) Their garments indicate they have been redeemed (cf. 3:18). (g) Perhaps as determinative of all is the fact that they are crowned. *Only* saints of the church age are promised crowns as rewards. They have already received them, and that means the judgment seat of Christ has taken place (II Cor 5:10). The Rapture, let it be remembered, is not a reward; it is of grace just as salvation is.

4. Activity before the throne. 4:5.

5. It is significant that from and before the throne there are lightnings, thunder, and fire. Here the throne is one of judgment and not of grace. Judgment is pending and ready to break.

5. Four creatures around the throne. 4:6, 7.

6. The sea of glass is reminiscent of the laver in the Mosaic tabernacle and the bronze sea of the Solomonic temple (cf. II Chr 4:2-6). Holiness is now a fixed state, as in 15:2. Much discussion has centered about the four living creatures (not "beasts" as in AV). Some connect them with the four gospels, as did some of the early Church Fathers; others see in them the cherubim; still others consider them to represent the basic forms of the divine government. They are God's instruments for the carrying out of His judgments. They indicate the attributes of God and the principles of His actions represented by angelic beings. The fullness of eyes denotes omniscient perception of God in His judgments. All is under His infinite wisdom. Four is the number of universality (cf. Walter Scott, *Exposition of the Revelation of Jesus Christ*, pp. 125-126).

7. The lion represents power and majesty; the calf, endurance; man, intelligence; the eagle, speed in execu-

tion of judgment. The parallel with Ezekiel 1 is inescapable.

6. Worship by the four creatures. 4:8, 9.

8. Untiringly and without interruption they worship, ascribing holiness to the Triune God in the Trisagion of Isaiah 6:3. The eternality of the Godhead is emphasized again.

9. They so enter into the purposes of God, that they can praise and glorify Him for all that will proceed from His throne.

7. Worship from the twenty-four elders. 4:10, 11.

10. The church in heaven will occupy herself with worship, the highest function of any creature of God. In this exercise the rewards (crowns) will find their greatest use.

11. The focus and worship here center on the fact of God's claims as Creator. There is another basis upon which God can rest His judgments of man and creation; it is His right as Redeemer, a truth enunciated in chapter 5.

B. The Redeemer on the Throne. 5:1-14.

Chapters 4 and 5 are introductory to, and explanatory of, the remainder of the Apocalypse. This chapter carries on the scene from the previous chapter.

1. The book with seven seals. 5:1.

1. One must first disabuse his mind concerning the meaning of the "book," because it has no relation to modern book-binding. It was in fact a scroll, which was so full of information that it took both sides, front and back. Moreover, it was firmly sealed with seven seals, so that the contents could not be known until God's appointed time. R. H. Charles (*The Revelation of St. John*, I, pp. 137-138) states: "A will . . . in Roman law bore the seven seals of the seven witnesses on the threads that secured the tablets or parchment. . . . Such a Testament could not

be carried into execution till all the seven seals were loosed." The scroll was not a book of prophecy or even the Book of Revelation, because that would not require worthiness to open it. It is the title deed to the earth, to which Christ has the right of ownership, both by way of creation and even more by way of redemption at Calvary. The book was in the hand of the Father and is the same as that in 10:2.

2. The Lion of Judah and the book. 5:2-5.

2, 3. The strong angel is not further identified, but his question points up the dilemma connected with the book. No one of the angelic host or the human race or the demonic host could open the seals or look into the book.

4. The failure was not merely one of lack of power, but of worthiness. The book must involve a matter of importance for the apostle to weep so.

5. Weeping is turned to joy when one of the elders points out the One able to open the book and the seals. The designation of Lion of the tribe of Judah and the Root of David directly relate Him to Israel (cf. 22:16; Mt 22:42-46).

3. The Lamb and the book. 5:6, 7.

6. Notice that the Lion is the lamb (cf. Jn 1:29, 36). He will always bear the marks of His suffering and death in His glorified, resurrected body. He overcame as a Lamb (cf. Isa 53:7), and all can overcome through His blood (cf. Rev 12:11). He sits now at the right hand of the Father (cf. Heb 1:3), but in that day He will stand (cf. Isa 3:13). He was slain but is alive now forever. The seven horns point to His fullness of power (cf. Ps 88: 17, 24); the seven eyes speak of complete wisdom (cf. Zech 4:10), a characteristic of the fullness of the Spirit which was uniquely His. Thus, the Lamb's three qualifications are: (1) He was sacrificed for man's sins; (2) He has all power to overcome every foe; (3) He enjoys all wisdom and intelligence to foresee and oversee.

7. The act described here represents and includes all that the Revelation will yet unfold. It is that for which creation, that is, the world of humanity, and the church especially have been waiting through all the centuries.
    4. The worship of the creatures and the elders. 5:8-10.
    8. Now the prayers, symbolized by the incense, of the saints of all ages will be answered. It is the saints holding up to Christ their own prayers, those of one another, and of all the redeemed.
    9. They sing a new song, but it is the old, old story. The worthiness of the Lamb is clearly stated as a result of His work on Calvary, which purchased to God every trusting heart. Notice the three circles of praise (vss. 9-13). The redeemed in heaven are the closest to the throne, and from them praise goes out in ever-widening circles.
    10. Many claim the reign of the saints on the earth is a fancy. It is claimed that it is carnal and Jewish. The saints in heaven, who are made kings and priests (1:6), do not so regard it. That reign is not first spoken of in 20:4, because it has been stated in 3:21 in a promise and here in praise (cf. Mt 25:31).
    5. All creatures worship the Lamb. 5:11-14.
    11. Both in verse 9 and here a vast multitude of redeemed are seen in heaven. It must be noticed that the angels do not indicate they have been redeemed. They have been preserved, not saved.
    12. Sevenfold accrual is the Lamb's because of Calvary and the unfathomable agony endured there.
    13. Every area of creation — heaven, earth, subterranean, and sea — is included. Cf. Phil 2:10, 11. Both the Father and the Son are recipients of the acclaim.
    14. Now the four living creatures and the elders respond in unanimity. The psalmist was right: "Praise is becoming to the upright" (Ps 33:1).

4 The Seal Judgments

Chapter 6

Chapters 4 and 5 were occupied with heaven; in chapter 6 events of the earth, with which most of the Apocalypse deals, come before the reader. Here is presented the method by which the truth of chapter 5 is carried out: Christ's entering in upon the purchased possession. The Day of the Lord, the time of God's judgments on earth before the visible reappearing of the Lord Jesus, is the subject in this and the following chapters.

A. The First Seal: The White Horse. 6:1, 2.

1. At this point it is well to make an important distinction. When the Tribulation Period is spoken of, reference is to all seven years of Daniel 9:27. The Great Tribulation covers only the last three and a half years of the period. Expositors are far from agreement on when the latter part of the trials on earth will begin. The present writer holds that the final part of the Tribulation Period coincides with the events of Matthew 24:15ff. Thus the first six seals occur during the first half of Daniel's seventieth week. They are the beginning of sorrows (cf. Mt 24:8). The first four seals are broken in connection with the four living creatures, but it is the Lamb who has the power and authority to break the seals. As He does so, more of the contents of the scroll are brought into view.

2. The rider on the white horse has been identified with Christ (cf. ch. 19) or even a false Christ. To refer the rider to any specific person is not in keeping with the interpretation of the other horses, which symbolize conditions and not individuals. This rider and horse refer to the attempts of many to bring in permanent peace. Cf. I Thess 5:3. It is verifiable from many times in the past, and especially in this century, that before some of the greatest conflicts between nations, there have been powerful attempts at man-made peace. The text indicates the desire to conquer in this area, but does not state that the objective was achieved. Horses in this passage speak of the powerful providential actions connected with the government of the earth. Speed is also a factor (cf. Zech 1, 6). White speaks of victory and triumph, a bloodless victory for the moment.

B. The Second Seal: The Red Horse. 6:3, 4.

3, 4. The second living creature is connected with the breaking of the second seal. Unquestionably, this seal speaks of war, bloodshed. Man's attempts at world peace have failed miserably and carnage is the result. Cf. Mt 24:6, 7. The great sword indicates war's ravages will be let loose on a universal scale throughout the earth.

C. The Third Seal: The Black Horse. 6:5, 6.

5. A pair of scales in the hand of the rider is a symbol of commerce. Too, when there is abundance, there is no minute weighing of common articles of food (cf. Ezk 4:10, 16). Worldwide war is followed by worldwide famine (cf. Mt 24:7b), because the soil is abused and men are not free to work it as necessary.

6. The scarcity of the time is underscored by the inflated price of necessities. One man's meal of wheat will take a day's wage; in barley (the food for cattle and horses) three meals can be bought for a day's wage. These are starvation conditions. Wheat and barley are

necessities of life, but why the mention of oil and wine? They are luxuries (cf. Prov 21:17; Ps 104:15) for the rich. The wealthy will apparently not be touched at the first, but ultimately they will undergo suffering as well (cf. W. Scott, *op. cit.*, p. 150).

D. The Fourth Seal: The Ashen Horse. 6:7, 8.

7, 8. The livid or pale horse clearly speaks of death, probably by pestilence and plague. Death is the place of the body of the departed and is synonymous with the grave; Hades is the abode of the departed spirit (cf. Ezk 14:21; see Mt 24 for the same order as in the horses). Notice that one-fourth of the earth is involved. When in human history has such a pestilence overtaken man?

E. The Fifth Seal: The Martyrs. 6:9-11.

In verses 2-8 of this chapter the first four seals are grouped, and the remaining seals are conceived of as united. The providences of verses 2-8 have occurred in other ages also, but not with such severity as in the age of judgment under consideration.

9. The scene is now one relating to the temple, incidentally another indication that Israel is to the fore in these dealings with earth. The altar was the appointed place of sacrifice, because these martyrs had been slain as burnt offerings for the Word of God and their testimony. John on Patmos could understand something of their experience. The souls are the Jewish martyrs of that period.

10. Their cry for vengeance is in keeping with an age of judgment. "How long" is the well-known prayer of Jewish saints, so often found in the imprecatory and other psalms. These departed saints must not be confused with the saints of this age, who have already been seen as seated and crowned in heaven.

11. These souls are not unredeemed crying out for revenge on their persecutors. The white robe given to

each indicates they are justified and accepted by God. Then they are told something of God's counsels. They are to rest a short while longer until their brethren and fellow-martyrs of the last part of the Tribulation Period will have been slain. In grace God desires the witnesses of other martyrs to be added to theirs already given.

F. The Sixth Seal: Upheaval in Nature. 6:12-17.

With reference to this judgment interpreters are divided as to whether all is to be taken literally or symbolically. The best hermeneutical principle is to take all elements of a passage literally, unless such a procedure issues in conflict with other literal passages of Scripture and the demands of reason. Too, it must always be remembered that in the Apocalypse symbols and signs are normative and not an intrusion (cf. 1:1). The features under the sixth seal could well speak of literal occurrences, which in their universal effects must have social, emotional, and spiritual implications for all men involved. In these instances parallel passages are very helpful. Earthquakes, changes in the heavenly bodies, falling stars, and the movement of mountains and islands from their place are striking and terrifying phenomena of nature.

12. Our Lord has predicted earthquakes (cf. Mt 24:7); Isaiah had foretold the darkening of the sun (cf. 50:3); Joel had prophesied the change in the moon (cf. 2:30, 31).

13. The Olivet Discourse mentions the falling of the stars (cf. Mt 24:29 with Isa 34:4).

14. With such comprehensive upheavals in nature, no part of the physical universe could remain untouched. Earthquakes alone could be responsible for violent changes in mountains and islands, but in that day the phenomena will be greatly heightened in their effects.

15. How could society go on in an orderly manner?

There will be unsettling of religious and social forces. Human life will be in chaos and turmoil. But in that day there will be no escape.

16. None will be exempt. The terror will be universal. Notice that the cause of the miseries is not lost on those undergoing them. All understand that the trials of the Tribulation Period are traceable to the Father and the Lamb. The reference here is not to the judgment of chapter 20, nor is it a judgment of saved and unsaved alike. These individuals are beyond the day of grace.

17. They cry out, not for salvation or the intervention of God on their behalf, but for an end to their miseries.

5 A Parenthesis

Chapter 7

That there is a parenthesis or hiatus in this chapter is clear from a comparison of 6:12 and 8:1. This chapter does not carry on the episodes of Daniel's seventieth week in a chronological way. There is a break between the sixth and seventh seals. In the midst of wrath God remembers mercy for His own. Cf. Charles, *op. cit.*, p. 203.

A. The Sealed Remnant of Israel. 7:1-8.

All interpreters have seen two groups in this chapter, one in verses 1-8 and another in verses 9-17. In fact, they are so distinct that some have considered that they do not belong in the same chapter. But this is to disregard the unity of the portion.

1. The four angels are not prominent creatures or they would have been specified with more detail. They are God's providential restraining forces against judgment until the sealing is completed. Winds are known to be God's agencies to carry out His purposes (cf. Ps 148:8).

2. The angel in this verse is quite different by description and performance. Just as the seal today is the Holy Spirit (cf. Eph 1:13; 4:30), so it will be in the Tribulation Period. Only Christ can perform this sealing by the Spirit. He is the Angel of the Lord and the Angel of the Covenant of the Old Testament, another incidental proof the events are related to Israel's age. The seal probably includes a special impartation of the Holy Spirit for their

specific service for God.

3. In a period when ownership and security are vital factors (cf. 9:4; 14:1; 13:16) the seal of God on the foreheads of His servants is essential to their ministry.

4-8. Strangely, at this point there is much divergence of views as to the identity of the company in verses 4-8. Some take an allegorical interpretation, but this allows great latitude for the imagination and nothing firm upon which to rest. Some indicate the group must be the first-fruits of the church ("the Israel of God"). (Cf. H. Alford, *The Greek Testament*, Vol. IV, Part II, pp. 623-625.) Still others hold they are the Jewish nation in general. First, that they are of Israel is manifest from their identity (vs. 4) as trom every tribe of Israel. Second, they cannot be reckoned as the church, for that body is never called Israel (even in Gal 6:16, where the issue is legalizers over against genuine believers in Israel, who are the elect remnant in the church, Rom 11:5). Third, they cannot be Israel in general, for God would not place His seal upon unbelievers for service for Him. Finally, these servants are from the tribes of Israel, literally so, redeemed by God, and sealed for service when the church has been raptured to heaven (cf. 14:4).

As to the number 144,000, some take it literally and others symbolically. If symbolically, it appears strange that there is such a detailed enumeration of the tribes. If the number appears too small for the magnitude of the task, it need only be remembered that twelve apostles with godly ones in the church turned the world upside down in the first century (cf. Acts 17:6). That which has intrigued readers of the Apocalypse is that the enumeration includes Levi (he was never given a portion in the land under Joshua, only forty-eight cities in the territories of the other tribes); it substitutes Joseph for Ephraim; and most puzzling, it omits Dan. There is no ground for dogmatic assertion here, although opinions have been offered for the omission. One position is that Dan is omitted, because the Antichrist will come from that tribe, judging from Genesis 49:17. Such a view, built on so many imponderables, can scarcely be called valid. Notice also 49:16 is a strong promise. Another explanation is that Dan does not appear in the list, because it was the first tribe to embrace idolatry (cf. Jud 18). Nowhere is this serious departure from the Lord evaluated as worse than the idolatries of the other tribes. Moreover, in the distribution of the land in the reign of Christ in Jerusalem Dan is given his inheritance (Ezk 48:1, 2).

The time of the sealing is important if it can be determined approximately. Judging from the fact that the sealing is accomplished before the breaking of the seventh seal (8:1), it probably will take place before the last seal, thus before the second half of the Tribulation Period, when Satan's forces will be arrayed against the godly, and the witnesses will indeed need the added protection of God for their work. They are a special group for a specific mission.

B. Tribulation Saints. 7:9-17.

Again, various opinions have been advanced for the identity of this group. First, it can be stated with confidence that they are not the same group that is mentioned in the first part of the chapter. It is clearly set forth that this second company is from all nations of the earth, whereas it was clearly presented that the 144,000 were from one nation alone, Israel. To mingle the groups would be to confuse identities which the Scriptures are careful to distinguish. Second, they are not the church, because they are separate from the elders (vss. 11, 13). Third, nothing is intimated concerning death or resurrection, for they are probably (to be seen later) on earth. Fourth, they are redeemed, as indicated in verses 13 and 14. Fifth, the time of their salvation is after the Rapture (vs. 14). How they came to saving faith is not expressly stated, but the highest probability is that they were redeemed through the preaching of the 144,000 witnesses. Else, it is difficult to discern why the two groups are placed in juxtaposition in this chapter.

9. The multitude is innumerable, whereas the witnesses from Israel were exactly numbered, even with subdivisions in each case. They have access to the presence of God and the Lamb, clothed in the garments of righteousness. Moreover, the palm branches speak of victories over the enemy.

10. Their praise accords with the similar exercise of redeemed ones in this book.

11, 12. Angels, elders, and the four living creatures join in the symphony of praise to God.

13. One of the elders (since he is part of the church in heaven, he knows the answer, cf. I Cor 13:12), asked John as to the identity of the great company, evidently to focus attention on their essential nature.

14. If they are the church, it would be amazing that John could not recognize them as such. The elder identifies them as redeemed ones who have come out of the Great Tribulation (Gr *ek tēs thlipsews tēs megalēs*, out of the tribulation, the great one).

15. Where are these redeemed standing? Some declare they are in heaven; others, on earth. It seems that the second is the true view, because this verse mentions "in His temple," and speaks of serving "day and night." According to 21:22 and 21:25 of this book there is no night nor temple in heaven (cf. F. W. Grant, *The Revelation of Christ*, Part II, pp. 80, 81 *et al.*). Isaiah 66:19-21 teaches that there will be a temple in the Millennium and Isaiah 4:5, 6 predicts a tabernacle as well. Cf. for the details of

the temple Ezekiel 40-48.

16. See Isaiah 49:10. The reason many cannot conceive of these things happening in the Millennium is attributable to their lack of understanding of the glories of that wonderful age and reign, when the Lord Jesus Christ is visibly ruling the earth from His headquarters and capital in Jerusalem.

17. In view of the unprecedented agonies these redeemed have endured through the Great Tribulation, the words of promise in verses 15-17 are all the more welcome. The truth of Romans 8:18 will be found as true for them as it is for the church today.

6 The Seventh Seal and Four Trumpet Judgments

Chapter 8

When the seventh seal is opened, the entire scroll is open to view. The seventh seal includes the seven trumpets, a fact which would preclude the seal and trumpet judgments as simultaneous or concurrent. Apart from two parentheses (ch. 7 and chs. 10:1-11:14) the events of chapters 4 through 11 are in sequence. With the beginning of chapter 12, events are again viewed especially with reference to Israel and the chief participants of the last days of Israel's age. As for the bowl judgments of chapters 15 and 16, they appear to be the scroll reversed (cf. 5:1). It must be emphasized that the seal, trumpet, and bowl judgments are not contemporaneous, but successive. As events move on to a consummation, there is no marking time or retrogression.

With the seal judgments the mass of humanity on earth view them as providential acts only, such as have occurred in history before, although not with such severity. With the blasts of the trumpets, the judgments take on a severer and more judicial aspect. In the bowl judgments the concentrated and unmixed wrath of God is poured out. The trumpet judgments are treated from 8:2 through 11:18.

The Scriptures reveal that trumpets have in the past, and will in the future, accompany significant events. There was a trumpet at the giving of the law at Sinai (Ex 19:19). There were trumpets appointed in Israel for both worship and warning (Num 10:1-10); at Jericho the walls fell flat at the blasts of the trumpets (Josh 6:13-20); the Midianites were routed under Gideon when the trumpets were blown (Jud 7:16-22); and the Rapture of the church will occur at the blowing of the trumpet of God (I Thess 4:16 and I Cor 15:52). In the very nature of the case a trumpet is blown when something of great significance transpires, which must have widespread attention. Messiah's reign will be prepared for by trumpet judgments on the ungodly.

A. The Seventh Seal. 8:1, 2.

1, 2. With the breaking of the seventh seal no events are recorded. But an ominous silence pervades nature. It is indicative of the solemnity of the things that are about to take place. It is the calm before the storm. The half hour is not a reckoning according to a heavenly chronometer, but is indicative of a very brief period.

There are seven angels entrusted with the service of blowing the trumpets of judgment. Since they are not further described or commented on, there is no warrant to identify them with extra-biblical angels found in apocryphal books of Tobit or Enoch, who are named: Uriel, Raphael, Raguel, Michael, Sariel, Gabriel, and Remeiel. Speculation in such matters brings diminishing returns.

B. The Angel with a Golden Censer. 8:3-5.

3-5. This Angel is entirely separate from the seven angels mentioned in verse 2, not so much because of added description, but by the very nature of the work involved. It is undoubtedly the Lord Jesus Christ. The Bible knows of no other than He who does the work of mediating the prayers of the saints, symbolized by the incense (cf. 5:8). (Cf. Ottman, *The Unfolding of the Ages*, p. 201, and Lincoln, *Lectures on the Book of Revelation*, I, p.

137.) Again, it is vital to realize that altar, incense, and censer remind of Old Testament worship, another proof that attention is centered on Israel's (not the church's) age. He is not here functioning as the Advocate of church saints, because she is in heaven at this time. He is invoking the judgments of God on the oppressors of the remnant of Israel. In chapter 6 the altar was the bronze altar, because sacrifice of life was in view; here it is the golden altar, because intercession is referred to. This is the work of no mere human being or angel. (Other references where Christ is seen as another angel are 10:1 and 18:1.) There was no intercession in 6:9 but there is here; grace is needed by the living, not the dead. The prayers of the saints must be for judgment on their oppressors (in keeping with a time of judgment, but not in this day of grace), because this is the nature of the answer.

Fire, thunder, sounds, lightning, and earthquake all constitute a formula of catastrophe of universal proportions.

C. The First Trumpet Sounded. 8:6, 7.

6, 7. Once the mediating Angel has performed His work, the seven angels readied themselves for their important task. All interpreters express difficulty in explaining the trumpet judgments. The visitations do remind of the plagues of Egypt in Exodus, but the present judgments are much more severe and universal. Scott states (*The Book of the Revelation,* p. 188): "The interpretation of the Seals is a simple matter compared to that of the Trumpets." With the trumpets there is more of the element of mystery. The trumpet judgments, like the seal, are divided into two groups of four and three, indicating the number of the world, i.e., the four points of the compass, and the number of the Trinity. The last three trumpet judgments have the added designation of woe judgments because of their severity. Some interpret the judgments literally, which is the correct starting point hermeneutically, whereas the majority take them symbolically, a method impossible to rule out in view of the symbolical character of the Apocalypse.

As symbols, hail speaks of sudden judgment from God (cf. Isa. 28:2, 17); fire, of God's wrath (cf. Deut 32:22 and numerous other times); and blood, of death (cf. Ezk 14:19). The casting of them (they did not just fall) to the earth indicates omnipotent power behind it. The third part is referred to several times in this chapter, and has been understood as a reference to the revived Roman Empire of the end time, but there is insufficient evidence to be so specific at this point. Trees and grass have been understood symbolically of the high and low in society, but the literal sense is surely potent enough to convey horrendous decimation of natural elements so necessary for the ongoing of human existence on earth.

D. Second Trumpet Sounded. 8:8, 9.

8, 9. With the sounding of the second trumpet something like a burning mountain was thrown into the sea. It is usually held that the mountain is to be taken symbolically because of the expressed comparison (simile). To what is reference made? A mountain in Scripture is used to speak of a great kingdom power (cf. Isa 2:2; Zech 6; especially Jer 51:25). Some students of the passage have even named the kingdom, Babylon, probably on the basis of the Jeremiah passage. But with a minimum of Scripture characterization it is not wise to be so specific because of the wide range of possibilities. Seiss (*op. cit.*, p. 195), who takes the mountain symbolically, understands the sea as probably the Mediterranean Sea, the prominent sea of the Bible because of its position to the land of promise. If the sea is symbolical, it is known in

Scripture as a symbol of people in general (cf. Ps 2:1) and of restlessness among them (Rev 17:15). The trumpet judgment could well refer to a great upheaval in nature (as with the first trumpet) with disastrous results for the waters of the sea, making them unfit for human use, marine life, and commerce. Though in each instance only a third is involved, it is enough to disrupt life beyond recognition.

E. Third Trumpet Sounded. 8:10, 11.

10, 11. But the wrath of God is still not fully expended on the wicked of earth. Water is such an indispensable element of life that again waters and springs are affected, as the sea was under the second trumpet judgment. A great, burning star is seen falling from heaven. It is understandable that stars can be used of important personalities. Today there are sports stars of all descriptions, entertainment stars, and a host of others. Scripture uses the term symbolically of our Lord Jesus (cf. Num 24:17). Some interpreters find here an apostate ruler or dignitary, perhaps even a church leader, who falls from a high position. The symbolic explanation has credence because of the figurative name given the star. If so, then the contamination of the waters must indicate the corruption of the spiritual life of the masses. Wormwood (Gr *apsinth*), that which makes water no longer potable, is a bitter and poisonous herb. When used without control it can produce convulsions, paralysis, and even death. In fairness to all views it must be indicated that, if the falling star has reference to a celestial phenomenon, it is difficult to see how it could contaminate so large an area.

F. Fourth Trumpet Sounded. 8:12.

12. When earth, sea, ships, rivers, and springs of waters have been touched, there are other areas that have not been involved. Reference is to the heavenly

bodies. Notice once again the specific enumeration of one third. It is as though God in infinite patience touches just a part in order to bring to repentance before all is involved. Literal and symbolical interpretations have long vied for attention. Some who have explained the judgment symbolically have gone far afield into naming specific areas of land, people, rulers, religious leaders, doctrines, and much more. If taken literally, the objection has been that the obscuration of the heavenly bodies would not result in darkness for only two-thirds of the time. It may be pointed out that in Scripture certain signs and symbols go beyond the range of the natural (as the beasts of the Book of Daniel and the Revelation) in order to bring out certain revelatory truths. Then the symbols are admittedly arbitrary.

G. Announcement of Woe Judgments. 8:13.

13. The reading of "angel" (so AV) here is doubtless to be discarded in view of the strong testimony of Codices Sinaiticus, Alexandrinus, Vaticanus, and a host of eminent authorities (cf. Seiss, op.cit., pp. 200, 201). The eagle underscores the swiftness of the coming judgment (cf. also Mt 24:28). Ample warning is again given. So terrifying are the last three trumpet judgments that they have the added nomenclature of woe judgments. Once more, it is announced that the judgments are intended for those who have settled down on the earth (a characterization of the ungodly, cf. for contrast with 3:10; the verb in both cases is *katoikeo*, not simply *oikeo*). Man can never claim he has not been sufficiently warned of coming judgment. As with the judgment on sin in Eden, before the flood in Noah's day, and in every age since, God is infinitely patient and compassionate toward those deserving of His wrath.

7 The Fifth and Sixth Trumpets

Chapter 9

H. Fifth Trumpet Sounded. 9:1-12.

The last three trumpet judgments (called also the woe judgments) are equally difficult of interpretation as the first four. The last woe trumpet is to be found in 11:15-18.

1. The first of the woe judgments is directed from Satan against the ungodly in Israel (cf. vs. 4); the second is from the east upon idolatrous Gentiles (vss. 14, 15, 20). The star referred to had already fallen from heaven, the seat of authority. It appears to be the same as in 8:10, but here are added important details. It is the great apostate leader of the third trumpet. Some suggest it is the Antichrist, but to become specific here without further particulars is unwarranted. Why is a literal star not in view? It refers to a living person, because the work performed is that of a human or living being. A. C. Gaebelein (*The Revelation*, p. 63; so also Seiss, *op. cit.*, pp. 202-203) maintains it was Satan himself on the basis of 12:12. If it is a false teacher, then Satan works through him, as is clear from numerous other occasions in the history of mankind. The key to the pit of the abyss (so the Greek) was entrusted to him.

2. What is the pit of the abyss? Is it Hades (Sheol), Tartarus, or Gehenna? The full discussion of the phrase will be found in this commentary at chapter 20. For the moment let it be said that it is the detention place of

73

Satan and the demons (cf. Lk 8:31; Rev 20:3). When the abyss is opened, smoke as of a great furnace issues from it. The blinding affect of smoke is well-known; here it refers to moral blinding. Reference is to that strong delusion that leads to perdition (cf. II Thess 2:11, 12). Their whole spiritual horizon will be darkened by the false system let loose, obscuring the true light from God. All the apostate, pagan systems are leading to this dire situation, culminating in the Tribulation Period.

3, 4. From the smoke came forth locusts, which have power like that of scorpions. It is immediately clear that these are not ordinary, earthly locusts. They are symbolic, not literal, because they do not feed on the natural food of locusts, such as grass, greenery, trees; indeed, they do not seem to eat at all, but rather injure men. They do no harm to nature, but they torture men, especially the ungodly in the land of Israel (cf. vs. 4 last clause with 7:1-3).

5. Their function is, not to kill, but to torment. Here as in the Book of Job (cf. 1:9-12) Satan must operate within the authority permitted of God. The torment is for five months, a limited time. This is the natural life of a literal locust, that is, from May to September. The pain from the sting of a scorpion, though not always fatal, is generally so; it is perhaps the most intense that any animal can inflict on the human body. These forces with malign intent thus overrun the Holy Land and the unsealed portion of Israel.

6. So great will be the torment of those with sin-laden and guilty conscience, that men will seek relief in self-destruction, but suicide will be impossible. There will be no rest of heart or peace of mind.

7-10. Now follows a detailed description of these supernatural locusts. In their strength and irresistible onslaught they are likened to horses ready for war. Further, they will be victorious, for on their heads they wear crowns like gold. As to facial features they resemble men, indicating human intelligence. Another symbolic detail indicates their hair as copious as women in attractiveness. Lion's teeth remind us that they are fierce and rapacious in their destructiveness. Nor are they to be halted in their designs, for they have the protection of breastplates that are likened to iron. Stubborn resistance and impenetrable qualities are indicated here. Locusts would be expected to have wings, so these have them; but they are of such number and power, that they sound like horses and chariots rushing on to combat.

Fearful enough has been the portrayal thus far, but more is yet to come. As in verse 5 they are compared to scorpions with stings in their tails capable of inflicting excruciating pain. No dimensions are given for them, but judging from a size in keeping with the other details of the picture, they must be of extraordinary proportions. They have a certain degree and measure of intelligence, because they do not hurt the ones with the seal of God and they are able to understand and execute commands given them. They combine characteristics of horse, chariot, lion, man, and scorpion. This full description is sufficient of itself to demonstrate that the locusts cannot be literal, but are symbolic. Mark you, they are none the less real for their figurative character.

11. Although locusts have no king (cf. Prov 30:27), these revelatory locusts have one, who is identified as the angel of the abyss. Moreover, this king's name is given in both Hebrew and Greek. Some interpreters believe the angel of the abyss is someone other than Satan, whereas others hold that they are one and the same being. Probably the latter is to be preferred; at any rate their objectives are undoubtedly the same. The names of this creature mean Destruction or Destroyer. Abaddon is first

because his blighting influence falls on Israel first, as in
the first woe trumpet (cf. v. 4). Apollyon signifies that his
judgment will next light on the Gentile world. The first title connects him with unbelieving Jews; the second, with
apostate Christendom.

12. The Spirit reminds that only one of the woe
judgments has been fulfilled; two others will be also.
I. Sixth Trumpet Sounded. 9:13-21.

13. The golden altar in the temple, and in the tabernacle as well, was placed directly before the veil, which
hid the holiest of all from human gaze. This verse is the
answer to the prayers of 8:3, 4. The voice is that of God or
one of His delegated messengers. The four horns are indicative of the whole strength of the altar of intercession
exerted to answer the prayers of the persecuted saints.

14. The four angels here are not those of 7:1-3. The
first (7:1-3) are at the ends of the earth; these of chapter 9
are in the limited region of the Euphrates. Those of
chapter 7 restrain; these do the opposite: they release.
The Euphrates is usually spoken of as the great river; it
is 1780 miles long. It will be referred to in 16:12. It is the
longest and most important river of Western Asia. It will
be remembered that the River of Egypt (the Wadi el
Arish) and the Euphrates are the bounds of the promised
land (cf. Gen. 15:18). The Euphrates was the boundary of
the eastern powers and of the old Roman Empire.

15. A specific time had arrived in the counsels of
God; with Him all proceeds on proper schedule. The mission on which the four angels are sent is to accomplish a
vast carnage.

16, 17. The number of the armies (cf. Ps 68:17) is
200,000,000. It is an immense army beyond calculation.
John did not count them, but he was told their number.
The armies of horses and horsemen will be involved in
waves of invasions. The horses evidently have riders

upon them, but the horsemen are not of primary importance, only to state the protection for their bodies. The
heads of the horses are compared to those of lions, and
from their mouths issue fire, smoke, and sulphur. The fire
will burn and smoke and brimstone (sulphur) will choke
and stifle to death. The combination here has been called
the "defensive armor of hell." Jacinth (hyacinth) is a deep
blue like that of a flame, but it is the blue of the pit and
not the blue of heaven. Cf. Genesis 19:24 for fire and
brimstone in judgment.

18, 19. The fire, smoke, and brimstone are so deadly
that they are now called plagues. They decimate one-
third of mankind, a visitation not known in history apart
from the flood of Noah's day. But the physical havoc is not
all; symbolically, the smoke can indicate the moral,
blighting delusion of the pit. The teachings and lies of
Satan will be manifold. The serpent-like tails speak of
deceit and falsehood. The tails are described as possess-
ing heads, that is, they are intelligently guided.

20, 21. If ever human obduracy and perversity were
pictured, it is here. Those who are spared the visitations
just set forth will neither repent of their wickedness nor
their worthless idolatries which are totally useless. Verse
20 tells of their worship; verse 21, of their works. Is it
possible that boasted civilization will revert to basest
idolatry? It is unmistakably stated that it will. The second woe is far worse than the first, but there is no repentance. The ungodly are incorrigible in their murders,
sorceries, and immorality. Punishment does not soften
wicked hearts; only the love of God can.

8 A Parenthesis

Chapters 10:1 — 11:14

Just as there was a parenthesis in chapter 7 between the sixth and seventh seals, so now from 10:1 to 11:14 there is a parenthetical section between the sixth and seventh trumpets. There is a very brief parenthesis (cf. 16:15) between the sixth and seventh bowl judgments. This shows the orderly arrangement of the Revelation.

A. The Angel with the Little Book. 10:1-11.

1. Of primary importance is the identity of the strong angel. Happily, there are details which reveal that He is the Angel of the Lord of the Old Testament, the Lord Jesus Christ. He sealed the 144,000 (cf. 7:2, 3); He offered incense with the prayers of the saints (cf. 8:1-6); He is clothed with a cloud, a heavenly clothing; His face is brilliant as the sun (cf. 1:16); a rainbow rests upon His head (cf. 4:3); His feet like pillars of fire tally with the description in 1:15. Why does Christ appear in the Apocalypse as an angel? Is this retrogression in doctrine rather than progress? He appears as an angel, because reference is made to conditions in Israel before their Messiah had been revealed in incarnation to them. He takes the same position as He occupied in Old Testament times, another proof that the Tribulation Period is a part of the Jewish age, unfinished at the first coming of Christ.

2. Attention is next directed to the little open book in the hand of the Angel. There are three views as to the

identity of the little book: (1) It is the same book as the
seven-sealed book of 5:1; (2) it is the aggregate of Old
Testament prophecy concerning Israel (it is strange that
a little book could contain so much prophetic truth); and
(3) it is the part of the Revelation that is subsequent to
the sounding of the seventh trumpet (i.e., 11:19-19:21). We
prefer the first position (cf. also Ironside, *op. cit.*, pp.
175-176). The reason is that in a book of symbols it would
be confusing to have a detail in chapter 5 appear again in
chapter 10 with another meaning without some explanation. The reference is, then, to the title-deed to the earth.
Here He makes His indisputable claim to all creation as
His inalienable right. Further proof is forthcoming in the
Angel's action. He placed one foot on sea and one on land.
In the Old Testament such an act signified taking possession of that place (cf. Deut 11:24; Josh 1:3).

3. The voice of the Angel was like the roaring of a
lion, for He is the Lion of the tribe of Judah (cf. 5:5). A lion
always roars when he has caught his prey (cf. Amos 3:4).
In chapter 5 He was seen in the role of Lamb; here as the
Lion He is pictured in His wrath (cf. 6:16). Again, peals of
thunder speak of God's activity in judgment.

4. At this point John was about to record the import
of the thunders, but the Lord did not permit it. The manner in which all takes place is not revealed (cf. Deut 29:29).
In this book of disclosures this is the only detail sealed.

5-7. The solemnity of the transaction is underscored.
He swears by the God of all creation. What is the subject
of the oath? Simply, it is that there will be delay no
longer. The translation of "delay" (Gr *chronos*) as "time"
is unfortunate (so AV), because it is inaccurate. There is
here no announcement of the end of time and the ushering in of eternity, for that comes over 1,000 years later.
The Angel is stating, rather, that there will be no more
delay in rectifying the wrong government of the earth.

Sin has held sway long enough. God's secret dealings are over, and His public judgments begin. Heaven is silent no longer. Man's day is about to close. The seventh angel is the one who sounds the seventh trumpet. What is the "mystery of God" that is finished? Reference is to His permission of evil to go on in its present course with seeming impunity. God appears to be silent in the whole conflict between good and evil. According to a Jewish proverb, "Michael flies with but one wing, and Gabriel with two." In short, God is quick in sending angels of peace, and they fly swiftly. But the messengers of wrath come slowly. But they do come!

8-11. Now John is told to become actively involved in the unveiling of coming events. He is charged to take the little book from the hand of the Angel. The reply of the Angel in verse 9 reminds of the experience of Ezekiel in his ministry (cf. Ezk 2:8-3:3). The eating of the scroll is done by faith through meditation and reflection. To eat is to incorporate into one's being. Cf. John 6:49-58. The study of the prophetic word and its central emphasis on Christ and His ultimate victory has a twofold effect: a sweet and a bitter. It both gladdens and saddens. The truth of the Lord's reign and triumph was sweet to John, but the judgments and plagues by which that consummation will be brought about will be bitter indeed.

What is the meaning of the command to prophesy again concerning kings and nations? It will be remembered that only the first and second series of septenary judgments have been covered in the chapters thus far. There remains the last series (the bowl judgments) to be unfolded. Furthermore, there are other disclosures in chapter 12 to the end of the book concerning Satan, a final political leader, the Antichrist, the world system of godlessness, the reign of Christ, judgment, resurrection, and the new heaven and new earth. It is an approach to the subjects of chapters 1-11, but with many significant details added. The truth of the book is duplicated just as Pharaoh's dream of the famine (cf. Gen 41:32) was repeated to him.

B. The Two Witnesses. 11:1-13.

1, 2. Again, the mention of the temple of God, the altar, the court, and the holy city alerts the reader that events continue on Jewish ground. Yet there are some eminent students who claim that verses 1-14 are one of the most difficult portions of the Revelation (cf. H. Alford, *in loco*). Much of the confusion is attributable to the fact that they inject the church here, whereas she has been seen in heaven since chapter 4.

This chapter through verse 14 is the continuation of the parenthesis begun in 10:1 between the sixth and seventh trumpets. The background of chapter 11 is essential. The nation Israel is returned to their land in unbelief. They have made a covenant with a sinister political leader of the time (cf. Dan 9:27), who promises them political protection and religious freedom. The temple is rebuilt with an attempt at restoring the Mosaic ritual. It may be well here to review the status of the temple in Israel and then touch on a preview of what is yet in store. The tabernacle of Moses (cf. Ex 25 ff.) was the pattern, greatly enlarged to be sure, for the majestic temple of Solomon (cf. I Kgs 7-8). With its destruction in 586 B.C. by Nebuchadnezzar of Babylon and the subsequent exile, Israel was without a temple. More than a score of years were added before the restoration temple was built under Zerubbabel, a scion of the Davidic house, and with the spiritual motivation provided by the prophets Haggai and Zechariah near the end of the sixth century B.C. During the reign of Herod under Roman suzerainty the temple was renovated over a period of time (cf. Jn 2:20), only to be destroyed by the armies of Titus at the end of the Judaeo-Roman War of A.D.

66-70. Israel has not had, and does not now have, a temple in Jerusalem. Judaism knows only worship in synagogues around the world. (Reformed Jews speak of their places of worship as temples, but in no sense do they imply any relationship to the temples already discussed here.) When the church has been taken to heaven in the Rapture (an event that may transpire at any moment — "in a moment," I Cor 15:52), and Israel is returned to their land, they will build a temple in Jerusalem. It may be called the Tribulation Temple. The Scripture references are clear: Daniel 9:27; 11:31; 12:11; Mt 24:15; Mark 13:14; II Thess 2:3, 4; and Rev 11:1, 2. There is yet to be another temple constructed, and it will be built by the Lord Jesus Christ. It is the Millennial Temple (cf. Isa 66:20-23; Ezk 40-48; Zech 6:12, 13). In the New Jerusalem there will be no temple (cf. Rev. 21:22).

John's people are in view, so he is commanded to measure the temple, the altar, and the worshipers. The altar is that of burnt offering, God's first provision for Israel's drawing nigh to Him. The measuring reminds of Ezekiel 40; Zechariah 2; and Revelation 21:15 ff. Measuring conveys the concept of marking off for one's own possession. God does recognize and claim a godly, worshiping remnant in Jerusalem in the time of the Tribulation. The measuring must be symbolical in that the worshipers are included. The outer court, it is explicitly stated, is to be excluded. In the temples in Israel in the past this was the court of the Gentiles. Now it is indicated that the Gentiles will not only command this area as their own, but for forty-two months (i.e., the three and a half years of the Great Tribulation) they will overrun Jerusalem as well. During the domination of the beast and the Antichrist (cf. ch. 13) Jerusalem will not enjoy autonomy. The rejected court speaks of the mass of the nation in apostasy and rejection, as well as their being the prey of the nations. It is Jerusalem's greatest hour of agony.

3, 4. But God never allows Himself to be without a witness. The very period of the trampling down of Jerusalem will be the time of their testimony, i.e., 1260 days. Their clothing of sackcloth shows their afflicted condition over the spiritual desolation about them. Notice that they preach with authority. Since they are identified only by the description in verse 4, which is general indeed, various identifications have been suggested by interpreters. Some claim the two witnesses are Elijah and Enoch, who did not experience death in order to see death here. Others say Moses and Elijah. This has much to commend it in the light of Malachi 4:4, 5, and the nature of the works that they perform (see vs. 6 of this chapter). A good number prefer to think of them as a godly remnant in Israel and not two men, since two relates to competent witness (cf. Deut 17:6; Jn 8:17). Some indicate uncertainty in identifying the witnesses. It is admitted by the majority that the witnessing ministry and miracles are like those of Moses and Elijah.

Their function is stated in verse 4 as similar to the two olive trees and the two lampstands before the Lord in Zechariah 4:14. In that passage the reference was to two specific men, Joshua the son of Jehozadak, the high priest, and Zerubbabel the son of Shealtiel, the governor, one representing the governmental power and the other the religious. Through them were mediated the light and message of God to the people of Israel in those post-captivity days. The two witnesses of the Great Tribulation serve in a royal and priestly capacity, witnessing to the soon coming of the King of the earth.

5, 6. Too, they have power to accredit and authenticate their mission to unbelieving Israel. Miracles like those of Moses and Elijah will confirm their divine em-

powering. Israel will be in a state of slavery as in Egypt
(now under the domination of the first beast), and in a condition of apostasy as in Elijah's day (now under the delusion of the false prophet, the second beast, cf. ch. 13:1-18).
Because they testify for God, they will be hated of the
ungodly. But they will be invincible and immortal until
their ministry is completed. Notice the range of their
authority in verse 6: "to smite the earth with every
plague" and "as often as they desire."

  7-10. Once the testimony of the witnesses is completed, they will glorify God even to death, being slain by
the beast. This is the first mention of the beast of Revelation 13:1ff. He actually carries on warfare against them
until they are martyred. Evidently, the populace will assent to the work of the beast, because in their anger
against the two witnesses they do not allow the corpses
to be buried, an indignity of immense proportions in the
East. With satanic cunning and deception the beast from
the abyss has won over the masses to his position.

  Jerusalem is characterized mystically (not literally) as
Sodom, because of its wickedness, and as Egypt, because
of its oppression and enslavement of the people of God,
both names appearing repeatedly in Scripture as the objects of God's unrelenting wrath. Lest any reader
misunderstand the geographical place intended because
of the use of symbolism, the passage identifies the place
as Jerusalem, where their (and our) Lord was crucified.
That Christ is designated as their Lord is proof that the
two witnesses are not representative of masses of individuals, nor are they angelic beings. They are redeemed men on earth.

  The three and a half days of verse 9 are literal days, ob-
viously. Now the utter depravity of the dwellers on earth
is manifested. They refuse decent burial for the
witnesses; but even more, they want to celebrate the

cessation of that witness which was so irksome and
tormenting to them in their incorrigible godlessness.
They will carry out merriment in feasts, banquets, and
exchange of gifts, so galling had been the testimony of the
godly messengers.

11-13. But the hour of vindication arrives at last.
Their indecent merriment would redound upon the heads
of the insensitive wicked. The witnesses are resurrected,
and that in the sight of all their enemies. But even more, a
heavenly voice calls them into the presence of the Lord;
they are afforded an ascension in the presence of their
foes. What an honor! Even Paul and the apostles were not
so rewarded. Furthermore, a final stroke of God's
displeasure is experienced by the ungodly. An earthquake, at the very hour of the ascension of the witnesses,
strikes the City of Jerusalem with lethal results; 7,000
people are slain in the disaster. Even the blindest
spiritually could not escape the meaning of the earthquake and the decimation of the population. The rest
mentioned are those who were spared. Their reaction
was terror; it was the result of human fear with no practical outcome. Outwardly, they give glory to God, but
their hearts are not genuinely touched, as future events
clearly attest.

C. Announcement of Third Woe. 11:14.

14. The parenthesis which began with 10:1 ends here.
It further confirms that the reader is not to expect an im-
provement or amelioration in conditions on earth, for
without change in men's hearts God's righteous
judgments must continue. Six trumpet judgments (including two woes) are concluded; there remains only fearful looking forward of more judgment, especially the
seventh trumpet or third woe visitation.

9 The Seventh Trumpet (Third Woe)

Chapter 11:15-19

15. Verses 15-18 return to the trumpet judgments, last dealt with at 9:21. It is immediately evident that under this trumpet many particulars of the events of the Tribulation Period are not treated. Verse 19, it is generally agreed, belongs to the next chapter and the additional details in the subsequent chapters. The seventh seal and the seventh trumpet are similar in that no judgment is directly announced under them (cf. 8:1; 11:15-18). Nothing is spoken of as coming from the sounding of the seventh trumpet; it is wrapped in silence. But loud voices in heaven have a vital declaration to make before the details of the last trumpet are revealed in the seven bowls of wrath in chapter 16. The heavenly announcement proclaims that the kingdom of the world (Gr *basileia* is singular, not plural as in the AV) has become the kingdom of the Lord Jesus Christ. The seventh trumpet does not bring in the kingdom; it only shows its proximity. The kingdom is in the singular, because under earth's final sinister political leader there will be an amalgamation of all kingdoms into one universal kingdom. Christ's reign will be eternal. If His rule is eternal, then how can it be a thousand years, millennial reign? He rules a thousand years (cf. 20:1-7) in time to vindicate and execute God's purposes for earth, then that kingdom is merged into the eternal kingdom. Verse 15 speaks of the kingdom an-

ticipatively as in preview, for the actual realization is to be seen in chapters 19 and 20.

16-18. As in chapter 4 the elders, the church in heaven, are seen worshiping the worthy God. Unstinted praise is rendered that God has finally consummated events on earth and reigns in omnipotence. So certain is it that it is spoken of as already accomplished. Now five significant factors are indicated as being fulfilled at that time. (1) The rage of the nations. They have exhibited defiance and arrogance against God many times before, but now it has reached its culmination (cf. Ps 2; Rev 16:13-16; 19:19). Here is an epitome of Armageddon. (2) The wrath of God. No longer will the patience of God be manifest. The hour of His vengeance will have arrived (cf. Ps 2:5; II Thess 1:7, 8). (3) The judgment of the dead. This is probably a reference to the future Great White Throne judgment (cf. Rev 20). (4) The rewarding of the godly. For the church this will occur at the Rapture; for other saints it will take place at the resurrection of the righteous in the first resurrection (cf. Rev 20). (5) The destruction of destroyers of the earth. The reference amply covers those who carry out their diabolical purposes in the Tribulation Period. What a summary this is.

19. With this verse John resumes the entire history from a different viewpoint, i.e., that of the chief participants in the soon-coming events. A good number of scholars connect this verse with the next three chapters, thus making yet another parenthesis, from 11:19-14:20, before the unveiling of the bowl judgments in chapters 15 and 16. There is much to be said in favor of this position. God resumes His relationship with Israel (ark of His covenant, His temple), but there is still judgment ahead as evidenced by the lightning, thunder, earthquake, and hailstorm.

10 Chief Participants in the Tribulation

Chapters 12, 13 and 14

From chapter 12 on, a new beginning and fuller details are presented. Chapters 12-14 constitute a connected and important prophecy in the book. Chapters 12 and 13 depict the principal agents for good and evil in the end time. Chapter 14 gives the consummation preparatory to the setting up of the kingdom. From 12:5 to 14:20 a great sweep of history is covered from the birth of Christ to the time of His treading the winepress of God's wrath. In the twelfth chapter alone, there is a grouping of events second to none in this book. The chapter takes the reader farther back than any other in the Revelation.

A. The Woman, the Red Dragon, and the Child. 12:1-6.

1, 2. The great sign is something pointing to a definite subject or object. The woman is actually on earth, but the sign is seen in heaven, so that God's purposes concerning her may be made known from heaven. Two distinct features are indicated concerning her: her clothing and her condition. She is clothed brilliantly with the heavenly bodies and a crown; she is a mother with child and in labor. When the Revelation is studied, it will be seen that the book pictures four women, all of them in a representative capacity. In 2:20 the woman Jezebel was seen, not in her individual and historic position, but as representing the clerical system at its highest, i.e., the papal system. In 17:1 the great harlot, as will be shown later, is all corrupt, apostate religious systems, especially professing Christendom. The bride, the church in heaven, is indicated in 19:7.

The fourth woman is the one under consideration in 12:1, 2. Various views have been put forth as to her identity. There are three positions as follows: (1) she is the virgin Mary. Nowhere in Scripture is Mary pictured as in verse 1. She is not portrayed in the gospels as verse 4 indicates. There is no biblical ground to believe Mary underwent the experience of verse 6. Moreover, how could verse 17 apply to her? She does not fit the picture.

(2) She is the church. This view has many adherents and defenders. H. Alford (*op. cit., in loco*); Matthew Henry (*Commentary*, VI, 1160); J. A. Seiss (*in loco*) represent this view with numerous others. The difficulty here is that the church did not give birth to Christ; He is the builder of the church (cf. Mt 16:18) and its foundation (cf. I Cor 3:11).

(3) Many hold the woman is Israel. A. T. Robertson (*op. cit., in loco*) holds that John must have had Isaiah 7:14 in mind. Even more, he knew, under the direction of the Spirit, Isaiah 9:6; 66:7, 8; Micah 5:2; and Romans 9:4, 5. The sun, moon, and stars indicate a complete system of government and remind the reader of Genesis 37:9. God had caused royal dignity to rest in Israel in the line of David. The number twelve appears with the twelve patriarchs, twelve disciples, and twelve thrones (cf. Mt 19:28). In verse 1 Israel is seen, not as she has been or is now, but as she will be. It is the nation as God had intended her to be, a condition that will be fulfilled in the reign of her Messiah. When the child, who is Christ, was born, the people of Israel were not in a place of power and dignity, but under the galling yoke of Roman domination.

3, 4. The scene now shifts to heaven where another sign is focused upon. The symbol is a great red dragon. It is called great, because it is not a minor or insignificant creature. He has great power. He is red, because he is eager and ready to shed blood. A dragon is a winged (for speed) serpent (for deception). The figure is meant to bear out great cruelty and hatred. Undoubtedly, this is Satan (cf. vs. 9 and 20:2). This is the first place in the Bible where Satan is called a dragon. But the description is enlarged: (1) he has seven heads, (2) ten horns, and (3) seven diadems. Some try to connect the seven heads with the seven great world monarchies of Egypt, Assyria, Babylon, Persia, Greece, Rome, and the Roman Empire in its restored condition (cf. J. A. Seiss, *op. cit.*, *in loco*). This is artificial and arbitrary, for the seventh kingdom is not a separate one from the Roman Empire of history. A head is a symbol of wisdom; seven speaks of fullness and completion. Satan is indeed wise and powerful. Horns represent power in Scripture (cf. I Sam 2:1; Zech 1:18-21; especially Dan 7:7, 8, 24, 25; Rev 13:1; 17:3, 12-16). Ten is the number of universality, and the goal of Satan is nothing less than world domination. Such is his objective, as will be seen in chapter 13. The seven diadems indicate Satan's objective to be crowned; he would reign over all men at all costs.

The tail symbolizes delusive power (cf. Isa 9:15), which Satan uses to accomplish the moral ruin of those in highest position. But he is not successful with all, only a third. Upon whom was the venom of Satan to be poured out? The answer is clear: the woman's child when He was born. Cf. Matthew 2 with Genesis 3:15. Herod was merely a tool in Satan's power, but he was nevertheless responsible.

5, 6. The identity of the woman and her child is placed beyond question in verse 5. The male child is to rule (Gr *poimainō*, to shepherd) all nations with a rod of iron; He is unmistakably the Lord Jesus Christ (cf. Ps 2:7,

9). As the Son of man He has sovereign rights of world rulership (cf. Ps 8; Dan 7:13, 14). What is remarkable is that the entire period in the life of Christ from His birth until His ascension is omitted here. But, as has been seen many times in Scripture, the record contains not only history but divine history and that from a specific viewpoint. History as such is not the aim, but the moral and spiritual purpose of God in the earth. The church age is omitted also in verse 6, because the purpose of God in Israel is the center of the book. What the woman in Genesis 3 was not able to accomplish, namely, victory over Satan, the woman here did effect in her all-victorious ascended Lord.

Again, a large span of history is not mentioned, that is, from the ascension of the Saviour to the flight of Israel in the Tribulation Period. Here is proof again that from the vantage point of the Old Testament the entire church age is an unrevealed mystery (cf. Eph 3:1-7). The same satanic fury unleashed at the birth of Christ is still operative against the godly of the nation that gave Him birth. The same faithful Father, who watched over His people in the time of the Saviour's birth, provides a place and nourishment from the relentless fury of the dragon. A wilderness is a place lacking human resources. It may have reference to Ezekiel 20:35, but there is no valid reason that it cannot refer to the literal wilderness east of the holy city, Jerusalem. The time is the latter half of of the Tribulation (1,260 days), what Daniel refers to as the "final period of the indignation" (or "the last end of the indignation" of the AV) of Daniel 8:19. Chronologically, verses 7-12 occur before the flight of the woman into the wilderness and explain, at least in part, the reason for the flight.

B. War in Heaven. 12:7-17.

This conflict is not said to be a sign, because the

presence of Satan in heaven is a reality (cf. Eph 6:10-12). Here is depicted the first step in the execution of the final judgment on Satan.

7, 8. In this section of the chapter another important personality of the Tribulation is introduced, namely, Michael the archangel. Notice these features: (1) his name. It means "Who is like God?" This bears testimony to the uniqueness of the God he serves. (2) He is clearly designated as "the archangel" (cf. Jude 9). Nowhere in Scripture is there a plural to this noun (cf. I Thess 4:16; Jude 9). (3) He has the added description of "the great prince" (cf. Dan 12:1). (4) He has power even to challenge Satan (cf. Jude 9). (5) He has angels at his command (cf. Rev 12:7). (6) He will be present at the Rapture of the church (cf. I Thess 4:16). (7) He is the champion of Israel and the espouser of their cause (cf. Dan 12:1; Rev 12:7). He appears when they are in question, and their interests are involved. His presence immediately alerts the reader the events relate to Israel and her enemies.

It is unusual to read of war in heaven, a place where peace and bliss prevail. But here the ultimate doom of Satan must begin, just as his first sin did (cf. Isa 14:12-14; Ezk 28:12-15). In pre-time his early fall was from the immediate presence of God to the second heaven (cf. Eph 6:10-12). Just as Michael has a retinue of angels at his command, Satan has his followers. The battle will be no dress rehearsal or sham encounter; it will be mortal conflict. But Satan, already defeated at Calvary, is no match for Michael and his angels. The weaker foe will be permanently dislodged, never to regain access to heaven. Doubtless, Christ foresaw this in Luke 10:17, 18. Satan's forceful eviction from heaven is a chief cause of the Great Tribulation. The three steps in Satan's ultimate doom are in 12:9; 20:3; and 20:10.

9. Twice it is stated that Satan was cast down, and

once concerning his angels. Now he will be identified to the full. First, he is the great dragon. Here power and cruelty are to the fore. Second, as serpent he is the master of cunning as with Eve in Eden. The "ancient" or "original" added characterization directly relates him to Genesis 3. "Devil" in the Greek conveys the force of slanderer or false accuser. Recall his blasphemous insinuations concerning God in tempting Eve. "Satan" means the adversary or opposer. All these attributes are employed in the one great objective of all his activities, namely, to deceive the entire world.

10-12. In the Apocalypse when earth mourns (cf. here and 18:11 with 19:1), heaven rejoices, an indication of how out of tune with heaven the earth is. The loud voice in heaven is not identified, but the message is filled with good news. The consummation of God's gracious purposes for His own draws nearer. Satan is called the accuser of the brethren, and he is tirelessly at his occupation (cf. Job 1:11; 2:5; Zech 3:1; Lk 22:31; see also I Jn 2:1 with its implications). The godly of all ages have been the target of his slanders. Surely, the 144,000 and the godly Gentiles (cf. ch. 7) with other redeemed ones of that time will be especially the objects of his unbounded fury for his expulsion from heaven.

The manner of the victory of the godly over Satan, different from the victory of Michael and his angels, will be threefold: the blood of the Lamb (their justification before God on that basis), their faithful witness to the work and grace of God, and their willingness to be martyred for their faith. No wonder heaven is called upon to rejoice. No earth-originated faith could accomplish this. But a warning woe is sounded for the earth and the sea (heaven now being inviolate without the sinister presence of Satan and his own), in view of the increased wrath of the devil because he knows his time is running out.

13-17. Verses 7-12 explain why the woman had to flee and why Satan is so furious on earth. In short, verse 13 resumes the thread of thought in verse 6. If further proof were needed, it is to be found in a comparison of the notations of time in verses 6 and 14. They treat of the same time, namely, the Great Tribulation; the 1,260 days are identical with the three and a half years. (Note: for purposes of computation the Bible reckons a year as 360 days.) It is clear throughout the account that the objective of the hatred of the dragon is the woman, Israel. What he could not accomplish at the birth of Christ, i.e., the extermination of the Saviour, he now seeks to compensate for by the persecution of Israel (vs. 13) and the remnant of her descendants (vs. 17).

But as the Lord undertook for Israel at the incarnation, so He does now. The wings of the eagle are known for their strength; here they represent God's enablement of the godly in Israel (perhaps the result of the witness of the 144,000 among them also). In Exodus 19:4 God indicated to Israel that He had borne them on eagles' wings and brought them into the wilderness from the hostile Egyptians; here He will grant them eagles' wings to flee from Jerusalem to the wilderness to escape the deadly venom of their archenemy Satan. His past faithfulness is a pledge of His fidelity in the then present hour. Nourishment (same as in vs. 6) will be afforded her in her extremity. Since the eagles' wings are intended symbolically in Exodus and in this passage, they may refer to friendly persons and nations who will espouse the cause of Israel.

However, Satan does not relinquish his evil schemes so easily. He now in a final desperate thrust tries to engulf the godly in Israel as by a river. Continuing the symbolism, this may refer to Satan's activating hostile nations on earth against the Jews. Again, he will be foiled by the alertness and activities of those who come to

Israel's aid. Defeated repeatedly, Satan's rage will be unbounded. His goal now is to annihilate the remnant who
remained in Jerusalem. That they are redeemed ones is
manifest from the characterization of them in the last
words of the chapter.

C. The Beast from the Sea. 13:1-10.

The apostle continues in this chapter the delineation of
the chief participants of the end time, adding two more to
the ones given in chapter 12. A study of Daniel 7, 9, and 11
is essential to the understanding of this vital chapter of
the Apocalypse.

1. In 19:20 the two beasts of this chapter are
designated as the Beast and the False Prophet. With the
dragon (vs. 2) they form a horrendous trio of evil. The
beasts are the chief wicked instruments of Satan. Here is
the culmination of the world's desire for the amalgamation and merger of political power and religious power, a
combination of church and state. The Roman Beast and
the Antichrist (man of sin of II Thess 2:3) will fulfill the
longing of the ungodly.

The better manuscripts read "he stood" instead of "I
stood" in verse 1. It is still the dragon spoken of in
chapter 12. He stands on the seashore in order to
motivate the rise of the beast from the sea. The verse
gives first the origin of the beast and then a general
description of his appearance. The sea in Scripture
represents multitudes of nations in tumult and unrest (cf.
Ps 2:1; Rev 17:15; 20:8). Interpreters of the Revelation differ as to the identity of the two beasts of this chapter.
Some hold that the first beast (vss. 1-10) is the Antichrist,
a political leader, and the second beast (vss. 11-18) is an
apostate Jew, a religious leader (cf. F. C. Ottman, op. cit.,
p. 321 f.). Others maintain that the first beast is the
Roman Beast, a political leader, and the second beast is

the False Prophet or Antichrist (cf. *New Scofield Reference Bible*, p. 1364, fn. 2; H. A. Ironside, *op. cit.*, pp. 219-235 and pp. 236-252). As the commentary proceeds, it will be seen that this writer holds to the latter view.

The first beast represents the revived Roman Empire (vs. 3), the ten toes of Daniel 2, which have not been historically fulfilled. So united with Satan is this beast-like leader, that what is written of Satan in 12:3 is here ascribed to the political leader. Cf. Daniel 7:8.

2. This verse throws much light on Daniel 7:1-12. There the first beast was a lion (eagles' wings are added to bring out added truth), namely, Babylon; the second was a bear, that is, Medo-Persia; the third was a leopard (birds' wings and heads are included to set forth additional truths), i.e., Greece. The fourth beast is not likened to any known animal in nature, hence is called the nondescript. Now it is clear why the fourth beast is not named, because there is no beast that combines the features of a leopard, bear, and lion. But the revived Roman Empire will incorporate the features of the preceding three empires. Ancient Rome boasted that, no matter how many powers she subjugated in her conquests, she could always assimilate them into her hegemony. That political power is being emphasized is certain from the mention of power, throne (i.e., the whole earth), and great authority.

3. Rome did suffer political decline. The city of Rome fell in A.D. 476 and to this hour the Roman Empire has ceased to exist. But it will rise again as this chapter reveals. Since World War II and Churchill's statement concerning the United States of Europe, there have been strong currents to build a confederation of nations in Europe as a sort of buffer between the superpowers of the East and West. Ten kingdoms will arise in western Europe (cf. 17:12). The ancient Roman Empire never ex-

isted in this form. It will be a strong attempt for a centralized power (17:13). The ruler over the federated kingdoms will be the little horn of Daniel 7:8 (cf. also Dan 9:27). The first beast of chapter 13 is the little horn (signifying political power) of Daniel 7:24, 25. Because the turn of events will be beyond normal expectation, the whole world will be astounded and, feeling there is the exhibition of supernatural power, will give their allegiance to the beast. Their wonder turns to worship, because the world has not witnessed such a sight as the revived Roman Empire. Once more Satan attempts to usurp God's place.

4. Realizing that the political leader is exercising power delegated from Satan, the world turns to worship the source of that authority. In doing so they ascribe to the beast omnipotence and invincibility. The insolent questions are to be answered in 19:11-16.

5. Notice that here and in verse 7 the words "given to him" occur four times. All is under the permissive direction of God as with Job and Satan long ago (cf. Job 1, 2). Only arrogance and blasphemous utterances issue from the mouth of this beast (also vs. 1, "blasphemous names"). Cf. Daniel 7:8, 11, 20, 25. So important is this latter part of the Tribulation Period, called the Great Tribulation (cf. 7:14), that in this chapter it is referred to explicitly by days (vs. 6), years (vs. 14), and months (here).

6. Blasphemy by definition is irreverent speech against God, but this beast is not satisfied with maligning God and His blessed character. He includes as well all the saints who are with the Lord in heaven. How could he have failed to realize the import of the great event of the Rapture of the church?

7. As Daniel had prophesied (cf. 7:21, 22), this vile political leader was permitted to wage war against the

saints still living on earth. Notice the wide range of his authority; in verse 15 he is enabled to kill all who do not worship his image.

8. With the display of such unprecedented power it is easy to see how all earth-dwellers (cf. 3:10; 13:12) will be quick to enlist themselves as worshippers of him. The times of the Gentiles began with man-worship (cf. Nebuchadnezzar in Dan 3) and they will end the same way, as is clearly stated here. Only those who have trusted Christ as Saviour, whose names are eternally recorded in the Lamb's book of life, will refuse the beast the worship that belongs only to God. If occurrences foretold here seem incredulous, let it be remembered that the deification of Roman emperors in the past is well-attested in history. They assumed divine titles, commanded divine honors, and built temples for the worship of themselves.

9, 10. The sway of the beast will be worldwide, so the call to hear is similarly broad. Retributive justice will be experienced in that day. The godly on earth in that day, especially the remnant in Israel, are called upon to refrain from employing carnal weapons (cf. the three witnesses in Dan 3). God's saints must endure patiently, thus exhibiting their sole faith in God.

D. The Beast from the Earth. 13:11-18.

The first beast comes from the sea, hence a Gentile; the second has his origin from the earth (or land) or the land of promise. As indicated earlier in this chapter, those who identify this beast with the Antichrist (which is the position of this writer) claim the second beast is an apostate Jew. Is this conclusion a compelling one as to his national origin? It is true that Jews would not accept as their Messiah a non-Jew, and history witnesses that they have received some scores of false Messiahs already (cf. Jn 5:43; Acts 5:36, 37). But the portrayal of the Antichrist in

Daniel 11:36-45; Zechariah 11:15-17; Matthew 24:15-28;
John 5:43; II Thessalonians 2:1-12; and here in Revelation
is such that the one called "the man of sin" is not likely to
be compelled by truth as to his national origin, any more
than he adheres to the facts in claiming to be God Himself
(cf. II Thess 2:4). Falsehood is one of the staples of his
stock in trade. Thus, he will arise from the land of promise and falsely claim to be of the nation of promise and
the promised Messiah.

11. Like Satan this beast, the third member of the
evil trio of the Tribulation Period, traffics in
counterfeiting. He has horns like a lamb; Satan's agents
are able to pass themselves off as messengers of light (cf.
II Cor 11:13-15). F. W. Grant (cf. *The Numerical Bible, in
loco*) has suggested that this beast seeks to imitate the
kingly and prophetic ministries of Christ. But his speech
betrays him as a tool of Satan; he pretends meekness and
humility as a lamb, but in actuality is a masterpiece of the
devil. He is stationed in Jerusalem (cf. II Thess 2:4), but
he owes his position and power to the first beast, who
resides in Rome (cf. Dan 11:38, 39, especially the words
"god of fortresses" and "foreign god"). With the military
help of his superior he can command universal compliance
with his demands.

12. As stated, the first beast is willing to sponsor the
Antichrist (he is also the False Prophet, cf. 19:20) with the
understanding that the coadjutor direct all worship to the
first beast. What a singular stroke of Satan that all this
transpires at the focal point of the world's three
monotheistic religions, namely, in Jerusalem.

13. Because God never sent a prophet of His without
proper attestation with miracles (cf. Moses and Elijah as
examples), Satan must counterfeit this feature also in
order to carry through the greatest deception of the ages.
Notice that the miracles are characterized as "great

signs," and one is specified which could deceive men into thinking that the Antichrist has power even in heaven.

14. It is known that a lackey will often overdo his role. So the Antichrist in working his signs commands that an image (idol) of the beast be made for universal homage. To this Christ referred in Matthew 24:15. It is the ultimate in man's search to be like God. Satan tried it; those at the Tower of Babel attempted it; now the Antichrist puts the finishing touches to the gruesome blasphemy. Cf. Matthew 24:24, 25; II Thessalonians 2:9, 10.

15. Even more, God permits a power which is not seen elsewhere in Scripture. The Antichrist wants to make the deception as strong as possible. So the image is given breath to speak, to command worship, and to mete out capital punishment to those who refuse adoration of the idol. When political power and man's religion are so wedded, Satan is indeed the master of ceremonies.

16, 17. All is despotic tyranny without consideration for divine or human rights. It is one thing to suffer social ostracism, or political deprivation, or religious persecution, but to link idolatrous worship with economic deprivation is a master stroke of Satan. Boycott is a potent use of force. In order to obtain the elements for livelihood it will be necessary to be branded in a visible place on the right hand or forehead with the mark of the beast, either his name or his number given in verse 18.

18. It is almost impossible to list the number of suggestions for 666, all the way from Nero in ancient Rome to persons in this day. Probably the most that can be gleaned is that, since seven is the biblical number of completion, six, which falls short of it, is man's failure at its worst. Man's worship of man is, indeed, spiritual insanity to the highest degree.

E. The Lamb and a Remnant on Mt. Zion. 14:1-5.

Chapter 14 is the sequel of God's answer to the wickedness of the persons in chapter 13. God intervenes in grace and judgment. As stated earlier, chapters 12 to 14 form a series of their own and are placed between the trumpet and bowl judgments, intending to emphasize the individuals prominent in the end time. R. H. Charles claims: "The entire chapter is *proleptic* in character. That is, the orderly development of future events as set forth in the successive visions is here . . . abandoned, and all the coming judgments from xvi. 17 to xx. 7-10, are summarized in xiv. 6-11, 14, 18-20" (*The Revelation of St. John*, II, p. 1).

1-5. All the persons mentioned in verse 1 have been before the reader earlier in the book. The Lamb is Christ, so designated by John as the favorite appellation for the Saviour. The Father needs no explanation. The 144,000 are undoubtedly those of chapter 7, the godly witnesses during the Tribulation, sealed and marked out for God. Mount Zion is the literal city of David, entirely consistent with the godly remnant from Israel.

The scene in verses 2 and 3 changes to heaven, from which comes forth a remarkable voice which sounds like many waters, loud thunder, and harp music. Who are the harpists and singers? By elimination it is evident that they are not the four living creatures, nor the elders, nor the 144,000 who had need to learn the song. The singing was done before the three already-named groups. Ottman (*op. cit.*, p. 339) suggests that they may be those who are martyred under the rampages of the beast. This proposal is as good as any other, because details for ascertaining the identity of these godly ones are general.

First, they are noted for their testimony; in their witness they were not ashamed to bear the name of their God (when puny, wicked man was claiming divine prerogatives) on their foreheads. Second, they kept themselves separated from the defilement of the world. The "virgins" of the AV (Gr *parthenoi*) is a correct, literal translation, but the connotations are misleading. There is no intent to advocate celibacy over against marriage (cf. Heb 13:4), but only to emphasize their chastity in life as virgins are. They have kept themselves from the idolatry so blatantly fostered by the Roman Beast and the False Prophet (ch. 13). Repeatedly in the Old Testament, idolatry is likened to fornication and adultery (cf. the Book of Hosea for an extended example). Third, they have chosen the highest fellowship in the universe; they are constantly in the company of the spotless Lamb of God. Fourth, they are honored to be firstfruits to God and Christ. The Lord Jesus is the firstfruits in resurrection (cf. I Cor 15:20); the church is the "first fruits of His creatures" (cf. Jas 1:18); here are the first fruits of the coming kingdom age (cf. Ironside, *op. cit.*, p. 256). Finally, in a day of wholesale falsehood and deception perpetrated by Satan and the Antichrist, these will keep themselves unblemished (not sinlessly perfect) by avoiding all lying.

F. The Angel with the Eternal Gospel. 14:6-7.

6, 7. In the next seven verses of the chapter three angels with different announcements are introduced. If voices are silenced on earth by devilish agents, God is not thwarted in His purposes to send forth His message to needy men. Gaebelein (*op. cit.*, p. 87) and Ottman (*op. cit.*, pp. 344-346) maintain that a literal angel is not in view here, but witnesses during the Tribulation Period who preach the gospel of the kingdom, that is, preparation by repentance for the coming of Messiah. The passage indicates nothing concerning the gospel of the kingdom (as John the Baptist preached it and the apostles as well before the crucifixion of Christ), but rather speaks of an

eternal gospel. Nor is there basis for assuming that the
angel represents witnesses during the Tribulation
Period. Moreover, this is not the gospel preached during
the church age for the purpose of gathering out a bride
for the Redeemer. It is specifically "good news" (Gr
euaggelion) of an eternal character intended for those
who inhabit (not the same Greek word as in 3:10) the
earth from all nations. Verse 7 seems to contradict the
concept of good news, for the contents appear to an-
nounce only judgment. This is a hasty conclusion. The
dual appeal in the message is to reverence God, giving
Him glory, and to worship Him as Creator of the
universe. Cf. Romans 1:20 with Psalm 19:1-6. This gospel
proclaims God is sovereign as Maker, and blessing is only
in obedience to His will. It is everlasting because it has
abided through the ages. It is in effect a call to come from
the worship of the Roman Beast, a creature, to God the
Creator. But the element of good news is definitely here:
the declaration of soon-coming judgment is made in view
of the time still granted to turn to God. If the die were
already cast, then the element of good tidings would be
absent, but such is not the case here.

G. Babylon's Fall Announced. 14:8.
        8. The second angel has an announcement unrelated
to any offer of grace. In broad outlines it states the fall of
Babylon the Great, who has seduced all the nations with
her immorality. Drawing on many Old Testament
passages, the reader is able to transfer the figure of
physical uncleanness to that of spiritual defection from
God to idolatry (cf. Jer 51:8). Interpreters differ on the
identity of this Babylon. There is a general consensus
that the Babylon introduced here proleptically is that of
chapters 17 and 18. R. H. Charles maintains that the fall
of Rome is announced (*op. cit.*, II, p. 14). Scott holds: "But

what is before us now is the mystic Babylon, that huge system of spiritual adultery and corruption which holds sway over the whole prophetic scene. It is scarcely possible to conceive of a huge system of wickedness eagerly embraced by the nations once called Christian. It will nevertheless be so. Babylon here is the full development of the state of things under the Thyatiran condition of the Church (chap. 2:18-23)" (*op. cit.,* p. 299). R. C. H. Lenski (*The Interpretation of St. John's Revelation,* p. 432), after designating the first beast of chapter 13 as "antichristian power" and the second beast as "antichristian propaganda," feels that "All those who do this constitute Babylon, *the antichristian world city or empire,* which is named 'Babylon the Great' after the Old Testament Babylon . . . the great enemy of Israel, Jerusalem, Zion." He elucidates further by way of summary (p. 434): "The preterists regard Babylon as a reference to pagan Rome alone; the historical interpreters as a reference to papal Rome; the futurists as a reference to the capital of the antichrist who is yet to come, either Rome or Jerusalem. Babylon . . . is *the entire antichristian* empire throughout the whole New Testament Era. Both pagan and also papal Rome would then be included." Since the mention of Babylon here is admittedly anticipatory to the detailed treatment in chapters 17 and 18, the entire subject will be dealt with at that place. This is the first mention of Babylon in the Revelation, but already her widespread influence and her wickedness are clearly set forth.

H. Judgment on Worshipers of the Beast. 14:9-12.

9-12. The third angel has a message of unrelieved judgment. Both verses 9 and 11 designate the objects of the divine visitation as the worshipers of the beast and his image and the recipients of his mark. The judgment depicted is horrendous indeed. It will be intoxication with the unmitigated wine of God's wrath, torment before the holy angels and the Lamb, and unceasing restlessness, namely, eternal torment. Those who hold that the unrepentant wicked will be ultimately restored to bliss (they are known as restitutionists) find no confirmation in verse 11. In fact, the words used in the New Testament for the eternality of God are found here (Gr *eis aiōnas aiōnōn*). Cf. 22:11 also. Their trust in the power and authority of the beasts (ch. 13) will not stand them in good stead in that coming day. Finally, as in 13:10 (last clause) perseverance and faith will be called for in the days when believers on earth are undergoing affliction and trials (W. Hendriksen, *More Than Conquerors*, pp. 186-187).

I. The Blessed Dead. 14:13.

13. It must be remembered that not all will share the experience of the 144,000 sealed ones. Many will suffer martyrdom in the period under consideration. Although it is always blessed to die in Christ (cf. Phil 1:21 with II Cor 5:6, 8), it will be peculiarly so in this time, for the blessedness will be near. Too, to die will be preferable to living, because they will be spared the remaining portion of the Great Tribulation. The alternatives will be either worship the beast and live, or resist him and be killed to die in the Lord. God will take full notice of their faithful works; their rewards are assured.

J. Reaping Earth's Sin. 14:14-20.

14-16. God's judgment of the ungodly on earth is now delineated under two figures: the harvest of earth (vss. 14-16) and the vintage of the earth (vss. 17-20). Careful consideration of the scene will reveal that the Great White Throne judgment is not in view here, but rather the judgment of the nations of Matthew 25:31-46, the tribunal at the end of Israel's age referred to in Matthew 13:40. The judge is the Lord Jesus Christ, as the portrayal indicates. Cf. 1:13; 10:1. The designation "a (not "the" for the Greek text does not have the definite article) son of man" identifies Him with the events of Daniel 7:13, 14, and all references to Son of man in the New Testament. The evidence of John 5:22, 27 is weighty. The crown speaks of His royal prerogative to judge. The sharp sickle can only remind of reaping activity. The sickle is mentioned only twelve times in the Bible, and seven occurrences are in this portion of the Revelation (cf. W. R. Newell, *The Book of the Revelation,* p. 228).

Notice that the angel of verse 15 proceeds from the temple in heaven, another indication that the age is related to Israel, not the church. Apparently, the angel conveys the signal of God the Father to the Son of man to begin the work of harvesting. No sooner is the will of the Father declared, than the Son performs it with obedience and power. The earth was ripe for judgment.

17-20. In verse 17 another angel is seen leaving the temple in heaven, and he is equipped with a sharp sickle. A caution is needed at this point. Some students of the book claim the reaping is of both saints and sinners. Surely, the entire context of the book would lead the reader to see that this Revelation scene is purely one of *judgment"* (Newell, *op. cit.,* p. 229). Fire in Scripture is a common figure for purifying by fire and as a means of judgment (cf. 20:10, 15, the lake of fire; God in His purity is likened to fire, Heb 12:29). The reference to altar has been found already in 6:9 and 8:3. Again, an angel conveys the message to begin the work of judgment, but this time it is not a reaping of a harvest, but the gathering of the vintage into the winepress of the wrath of God. Just as the harvest was ripe (vs. 15), so the grapes (vs. 19). Though the judgment in this chapter includes both Jews and Gentiles, verse 20 indicates where the center of events will be. The city is unquestionably Jerusalem. Instead of grape juice flowing from the winepress, it will be the blood of men. But the fearful picture is even more explicit; the blood will reach to the horses' bridles, estimated to be about four feet. Yet more, this river will stretch for two hundred miles (Gr *stadia*, i.e., the total of 1,600 *stadia* or furlongs). This is the distance from Bozrah (Edom) in the south (cf. Isa 63:1-6) to the Valley of Jehoshaphat at Jerusalem (cf. Joel 3:1-3, 9-14) to Megiddo in the north (cf. Rev 16:14, 16). It is generally conceived that Armageddon will be a battle; this stems from the translation in AV, RSV, NIV, and NEB of "battle" for the Greek *polemos*. This gives too simplified a picture of the conflict. The rendering in ASV and NASB of "war' is correct (cf. H. G. Liddell and R. Scott, *A Greek-English Lexicon*, Vol. II, col. 2), because the first meaning of the word is "war." Thus, Armageddon is not an isolated battle, but part of a larger picture of encounters in different parts of the land. The name of the war is called Armageddon, because the terrain there is better suited for warfare than anywhere else in the land. However, the climax of the War of Armageddon is at Jerusalem (cf. Zech 14:1-5, 12-15) with the visible appearing of the Lord Jesus Christ.

11 The Seven Bowl Judgments

Chapters 15 and 16

A. Preparation for the Judgments. 15.

The chapters now under consideration form a literary unit that follows logically after chapter 11, giving the third series of the septenary judgments of God. Why need there be three series of these judgments? They evidently follow the pattern of warfare as men know it: first, the initial encounter; then, the intensive assaults; finally, the consummating blows. Undoubtedly, the bowl judgments take place in the Great Tribulation in its last stages. The inference seems to be that they will transpire in a very brief period of time. They will be both rapid and severe. The Revelation does deal repeatedly with judgment but not exclusively so, for the final prospect is bright indeed.

1. Seven angels with seven plagues. 15:1.

1. In 10:7 it was stated that the mystery of God was finished, but no details were given. They are now seen in chapters 15 and 16. To introduce these fearful judgments called plagues, John is shown a sign in heaven (cf. 12:1, 3), which is characterized as great and marvelous. The concept of greatness is here, because in scope and intensity there has been nothing before this to compare with them. The idea of marvel is introduced, because the inflictions will excite amazement and wonder. These plagues are marked as last, because in them the wrath of God is fully

spent upon ungodly mankind.

2. The godly victors. 15:2-4.

2-4. Before judgment falls, John saw a company of victors with harps of God. They are the ones mentioned in 14:2, 3. Why the reference to a sea of glass? These who have triumphed over the beast (cf. ch. 13) have paid the supreme price and have entered into bliss. The sea may have reference to the bronze laver in the tabernacle of Moses and the bronze sea in the temple. Here its waters are not disturbed any longer; it is that which is unalterable and firm. Purity is indicated here, but it has been attained at the cost of trials under the beasts (so the fire). As in 14:2 they have harps to accompany their praise to God.

The theme of their harp playing is the song of Moses and the song of the Lamb (cf. Ex 15:1-18). What do these songs have in common? They both celebrate redemption and deliverance. In the first case, it was God's physical release of Israel from Egyptian servitude through the Passover Lamb; here it is liberation spiritually from the bondage of Satan and his agents through Christ our Passover (cf. I Cor 5:7). In their singing they extol God's great and marvelous works, His righteousness and truth, His sovereignty over the nations, His holiness, and ultimate reception of universal worship through the disclosure of His righteous dealings.

3. The temple in heaven. 15:5-8.

5-8. In order to underscore the holiness of God in His righteous judgments on sinful man, John is granted a view of the temple in heaven. Ready to perform their duties, the seven angels (cf. vs. 1) proceed from the temple fully equipped for their tasks. They are priests as well as angels, because their attire of clean, bright linen and golden girdles marks them as God's priests. Cf. 1:13 of Christ. Seiss has aptly indicated (*op. cit.*, p. 370): "They appear as priests, because they come for the sacrificing of a great sacrifice to the offended holiness and justice of God."

Notice how all is pervaded with gold, an emblem of the holiness and righteousness of God (cf. e.g., the cherubim of gold over the ark of the covenant in the Holy of Holies). One of the four living creatures at the command of God presented the seven angels with the seven golden bowls full of God's wrath. The "vials" of the AV (derived from the Gr *phialē)* is too weak to convey the idea that the receptacles were bowls, like those used for pouring libations in the Old Testament. (Cf. Zech 12:2 where the translation "cup" is inadequate; "bowl" is intended from the Heb word employed.)

The smoke filling the temple came from the incense of the priests' censers (cf. 8:5). Two attributes of God are now underscored: His power and glory. Where God's glory is manifested, man is unable to abide the sight. So it was with Moses (cf. Ex 40:34, 35) and in Solomon's day (cf. I Kgs 8:10, 11). So solemn and grave is the action that here no one is able to enter the temple until the plagues are finished (the chapter beginning and ending with the concept of finality and irretrievability).

B. Six Bowls of Judgment. 16:1-12.

1. Command to empty the bowls. 16:1.

1. It is quite instructive to compare the plagues of this chapter with those recorded of Egypt in Exodus 7:20-12:30. The voice from the temple is evidently that of God who authorizes the fearful final pouring out of His wrath on all nature and man. Notice throughout the chapter how the ultimate objects of the visitations are men (cf. vss. 2, 3, 8, 9, 10, 11, 14, and 21). Moreover, the increased intensity and range of the plagues are easily seen in this final series of God's dealings in judgment with ungodly men. In previous judgments it was usual to learn that the inflictions touched a third part of the earth; the

areas were limited. But no such restriction is recorded
concerning the bowl judgments. There is an unmistakable
finality about all the transactions. The pouring out indicates an overflowing measure without stint or reserve.
Bowls of the temple employed for purposes of grace are
now seen used for judgment.

2. Plague on the earth. 16:2.

2. The first visitation reminds at once of the sixth
plague in Egypt (cf. Ex 9:10, 11). The contents of this bowl
were loathsome, unsightly, and malignant (cancerous)
sores, which afflicted all worshipers of the beast and his
image. Ulcers will reveal outwardly their inner corrupt
moral and spiritual condition. Since no symbolism is indicated, the plague must be considered as literal as the
corresponding judgment on Egypt of old.

3. Plague on the sea. 16:3.

3. Under the second trumpet (cf. 8:8) only a third of
the sea was involved; here the picture is of the whole sea.
Some expositors prefer to understand the verse symbolically, but it is confusing to shift from literal to symbolic without some basis. Water, a source for the
sustenance of life, is here made an agent of death. So it
was with the water of Egypt in the first plague of Exodus
7:17-25. Immediately, all marine life died. Coagulated
blood is death-dealing and emits an unbearable stench.

4. Plague on the rivers and waters. 16:4-7.

4. Again, the similarity with the plagues of Egypt is
undeniable (cf. Ex 7:19-21). In 8:10, 11, under the third
trumpet only a third of the waters was involved; here
there is no limitation whatever. Water, an indispensable
commodity for life, is once more the object of God's judgment, as in verse 3.

5-7. It is interesting that so many subjects in the
Apocalyse have their special angel. The angel of the

waters has authority over this area of nature, and the judgment strikes his sphere of rule. But he justifies the judgment of God. God is as righteous in judgment as He is in blessing. Because men have poured our heedlessly the blood of God's servants, He operates on the principle of what the Latins termed *lex talionis*, the law of recompense in kind. It is attested to in numerous portions of Scripture. They deserved exactly the visitation God brought on them. Even the altar, symbolically to be sure, vindicates the wrath of God. There is evidently a connection here with the altar of burnt offering in 6:9-11.

5. Plague on the sun. 16:8, 9.

8, 9. W. Barclay has correctly stated (*op. cit.*, p. 165): "In Hebrew thought every natural force — the wind, the sun, the rain, the waters — had its directing angel. These angels were the ministering servants of God, placed by God in charge of various departments of nature in the universe." With the fourth trumpet judgment (8:12) the sun was darkened along with the moon and the stars, but only a third part of them was affected. Now, only the sun is touched, but in a totally different way. Instead of the sun being darkened, its rays were heightened in heat, so that men were scorched as with fire. The sun, the source of such blessing and essential to plant and animate life on earth is now a medium of God's wrath. Three times in this awesome chapter (vss. 9, 11, 21), it is declared that men reacted to their punishments with blasphemy against God, and not with repentance. These judgments are not remedial or corrective in effect, but reveal all the more the corruption of those undergoing them. The judgments are punitive; the dwellers on earth are incorrigible. Men who will not be drawn by God's love will not be attracted by His wrath.

6. Plague on the beast's throne. 16:10, 11.

10, 11. The fifth bowl judgment is poured out on the

throne of the beast. W. Hendriksen (*op. cit.*, p. 195) writes: "This throne of the beast is the center of antichristian government. Cf. Nah. 3:1; Hab. 3:12-14." Adhering to an undeviating symbolism, the result is generalities which leave the student of the book with few certainties of a specific nature. The throne of the beast (evidently, the first one of ch. 13) is Rome as his capital city. This plague is God's unequivocal answer to the insolent question of 13:4; that arrogance is further met with finality in 19:19-21. The darkness is another allusion to the plague of darkness in Egypt (cf. Ex 10:21-23). Gnawing of their tongues because of pain is the only expression of its kind in the Bible and speaks of the most intense agony and suffering. There is no repentance, but rather a further degradation. In verse 9 the name of God was blasphemed; here He Himself is derogated. Is there any question as to whether there will be repentance in hell?

7. Plague on the Euphrates River. 16:12.

12. This important river has been introduced earlier in connection with the sixth trumpet judgment. As noted earlier, the river is 1,800 miles long, from three to 1,200 yards wide, from ten to thirty feet deep. Usually, it is both deeper and wider (cf. Seiss, *in loco*). History records what hindrance the river has been to military operations. Reminding of the drying up of the Red Sea, this river will be dried up to allow passage of inimical forces into the Middle East area for the final conflict. The kings of the east referred to (Gr *apo anatoles eliou*, literally, from the sunrising) are the Asiatic lands like China, Japan, and the nations of the Far East.

C. Preview of Armageddon. 16:13-16.

13, 14. Verses 13-16 are evidently an integral portion of that which transpires at the pouring out of the sixth bowl. When verses 12 and 14 are compared, the conclu-

sion is compelling that the action of the first verse is
related to that of the second as cause and effect. Notice
the evil trio — dragon, beast (13:1), and false prophet
(13:11) — are out in full force, ready for mortal combat for
the final consummation. All three are characterized by
the same uncleanness and corruption. The unclean spirits
are not said to be frogs, but "like frogs." They are further
explicated as demon spirits who are capable of working
miracles, but of such magnitude and convincing quality
that they are capable of motivating and energizing, not
only the kings of the Far East but, the kings of the entire
world. What is the objective of this vast enterprise?
Simply stated, it is the summoning of all of them to the
War of Armageddon, captioned here as the War of the
Great Day of God Almighty. The mind can scarcely con-
jure up or fathom the scene and its vast implications for
the world of mankind. Compare for further light I Kings
22:19-38; Psalm 2:1-3; Joel 3:9-11; Matthew 24:24, 25; and
I Timothy 4:1.

15. Before a concluding word about this unparalleled
conflict, the Spirit indicates a parenthetical word in verse
15. It is Christ speaking and declaring that He is coming
as a thief. Nowhere in Scripture are believers warned
against the coming of the Saviour as a thief (cf. I Thess
5:1-8; notice how carefully the Spirit distinguishes
believers (sons of day) from unbelievers (sons of night).
Because of the intensification of demon activity, just
stated in verses 13, 14, the godly of the Tribulation are
warned against defilement from the widespread corruption, issuing in their shame.

16. There is no question that this verse carries on the
thought of verse 14, because the same verb (Gr *sunagō*, to
gather together) is found in both contexts. The additional
information of verse 16 is that the place of the conflict is
named in Hebrew, Har-Magedon. The conflict has been

foretold in various passages in the Old and New Testament (e.g., Ps 2:1-3), but now the geographical location is added. The more popular name is Armageddon (the Greek noun has a rough breathing equivalent to the letter H). Har is a well-known common noun for "mountain." Megiddo comes from a verb, meaning "to slaughter" (Heb *gadad;* its basic concept is to cut off, cf. KB, *Lexicon,* s.v.). The site was the great battleground of the Old Testament. It was the place of the victory of Deborah and Barak (cf. Jud 5:19); Josiah met his death before Pharaoh Necho in the Valley of Megiddo (cf. II Chr 35:22-24). Since the subject will be treated more fully in chapter 19 below, it will suffice to state that Megiddo is the mountain overlooking the Valley of Esdraelon (Greek for Jezreel), the great plain in the northern part of Palestine. Napoleon I is credited with having said of Megiddo: "What an excellent place into which all the armies of the world could be maneuvered."

D. The Seventh Bowl. 16:17-21.

    1. Plague on the air. 16:17, 18.

      17. When the seventh bowl was poured out, it was upon the air. This is the domain of Satan as prince of the power of the air (cf. Eph 2:2). Though cast out of the highest heaven in his pre-time rebellion against God (cf. Isa 14; Ezk 28), Satan has had access to the second heaven (cf. Eph 6:12; Rev 12:7). When cast down to the earth (12:8, 9) after his complete expulsion from the heavenly spheres, he could have limited activity over the air immediately above the earth. All this is with the authorization of God and in keeping with His holiness, "out of the temple from the throne." The voice from heaven utters one word in the Greek (*Gegonen,* "It is done") which declares that all God's plagues have thus been exhausted. (By contrast the word of the Lord Jesus on Calvary [Gr

Tetelestai, "It is finished" in Jn 19:30] has all the blessedness of a finished redemption for sinful men.)

18. Since all judgments are completed with this bowl plague, it is valid to see the remaining chapters concerning God's visitations (i.e., chs. 17, 18, 19), as summarized here. When the seventh bowl has done its intended work, all judgment will have been accomplished. Verse 18 easily reminds of similar expressions in 4:5; 8:5; 11:19. Cf. W. Lincoln, II, p. 86. Always there is an intensification of the trials and agonies. Yet more, an earthquake, such as had never been witnessed on earth, occurs. It is characterized by the words "great" (twice) and "mighty." Its scope, mark well, is unlimited.

2. The fall of Babylon. 16:19.

19. This is the second mention of judgment on Babylon (cf. 14:8). It is remarkable in that two chapters (17 and 18) are occupied at length with Babylon and her fate. In chapters 14 and 16 the city is described as great; the same is true of the portrayal in the following chapters. Expositors are divided as to whether the great city in verse 19 is the same as the Babylon of the same verse. They are definitely divided also as to the identity of Babylon, now mentioned for the third time in the book. One group of commentators equate the great city and Babylon with Jerusalem (cf. 11:8); others, with Rome (either political, religious, or papal). When reliable expositors differ so widely, it is presumptuous to be dogmatic. Furthermore, all would greatly desire more details for a final decision. As the reader of this commentary has already noticed, this writer prefers, as a principle in both extra-biblical and biblical writings, to understand the same subject of discussion unless there is clear basis for the introduction of another element. If the great city is other than Babylon, whose identity will be dealt with at length in the following two chapters, why is

Babylon introduced here without further introduction? Moreover, the catastrophe will strike not only Babylon the great, but the metropolises of the nations. J.A. Seiss sees a gradation in severity of judgment and doom: Jerusalem was two-thirds destroyed; the cities of the nations completely; finally, Babylon with the greatest onus of sin and guilt, suffering most poignantly (cf. *op. cit., in loco*).

3. Nature in upheaval. 16:20, 21.

20, 21. Verse 20 must not be made to teach the destruction of matter, which is neither biblical nor scientific. All that need be understood is that there will be a shifting and upheaval in the island and mountainous areas. Whether these changes are to be directly related to the earthquake mentioned in verse 18 (so H. Alford, *op. cit., in loco*) it is not essential to determine.

Hailstones have been mentioned before in the Apocalypse, but not such as are here indicated. Their magnitude and severity are emphasized. Each hailstone weighed about one hundred pounds. It takes little imagination to picture the destruction these would cause to houses and structures, and, most agonizing of all, upon human beings, especially children. Does man fathom the depth of his alienation from God and earnestly seek to be reconciled to his Judge? The more severe the judgment, the greater the blasphemy.

12 Judgment On Babylon

Chapters 17 and 18

A. Doom of the Harlot. Ch. 17.

That the theme of Babylon is an important one in the Revelation can be seen from the fact that the Spirit of God devotes two chapters in this essential book of prophecy to the subject. From Genesis 10:10 (Babel is from the Akkadian *Bab-ilu*, gate of God), which is the first mention, to Revelation 18:21, which is the last reference, this subject of biblical revelation and prophecy is given extraordinary prominence. The student of the Word of God is wise to stress what the Spirit underscores. All the so-called major prophets (Isa-Dan) have important disclosures concerning Babylon. Isaiah refers to the city some thirteen times, Ezekiel, some seventeen times, but Jeremiah most of all with one hundred and sixty-eight citations. In the Revelation, besides chapters 17 and 18 which are entirely devoted to the subject of Babylon, the first occurrence of the word is in 14:8; the second, in 16:19. Both passages indicate briefly the fall and doom of Babylon. In a true sense chapters 17 and 18 are an elaboration of 16:19.

Because so much has been written on the matter and so many differing views have been advanced, it is helpful at the outset to clear up certain positions. First, no student of the Bible, theological or otherwise, doubts that in historic times there has existed a literal city called

Babylon in the plain of Shinar. Cf. Genesis 10:10.

Second, large numbers of reverent students of Scripture understand Genesis 11 as teaching the inception of idolatry at Babel (Heb from *balal*, to confound, from which Eng "babble" is derived) and the confusion of men's languages (cf. Gen 11:7, 9).

Third, the city of Babylon was the seat of a great empire, dominating the ancient world from the fall of the Assyrian Empire with the capture of Nineveh in 612 B.C. until the demise of the Babylonian Empire through the capture of Babylon by Cyrus of Persia in 536 B.C. The city continued until about A.D. 100 (cf. ZPEB, I, pp. 439-448, art. by D. J. Wiseman). Today there are a number of cities, like Hilla, which have utilized the sun-dried and kiln-baked bricks of the ancient city to build new walls, houses, and dams (cf. Isa 13:19-22; Jer 50:23-26; 51:24-26; *Wycliffe Bible Encyclopedia*, I, pp. 187-190, art. by F. E. Young).

Fourth, it is well-known how idolatrous Babylon has been; both biblical and secular sources leave no room for doubt in the matter.

Fifth, it must be kept in mind that Revelation 17 and 18 are *not* dealing with literal, historical Babylon, so that the question of the rebuilding of a future Babylon is irrelevant in the interpretation of these chapters. Proof is forthcoming from 17:9 (Babylon was situated in a plain, not on seven mountains); 18:24 (such a wide range could not be true of literal Babylon); and especially 17:5, 7 ("mystery," which indicates something hitherto not made known, but now revealed, cf. Rom 16:25, 26; Eph 3:4-7. The import of the word is that a sense other than literal is to be understood). Cf. 11:8 where Gr *pneumatikōs* may be translated "spiritually" (so AV) or "mystically" (so NASB).

1. Her position. 17:1.

1. John the apostle/prophet is invited by one of the seven angels, who were entrusted with the seven bowl judgments, to witness the judgment of (1) the great harlot and (2) her position on many waters. The reader is not left to his own resources in the interpretation of this important chapter, but he must scrutinize every clue given. Harlotry is amply explained in passages of the Old and New Testament (cf. Hos 1-3; Ezk 16:15; Jas 4:4; II Pet 2:14). Both adultery and harlotry are sins of physical immorality which are made to represent spiritual defection and apostasy. Wherein her harlotry consists is explained in verses 4-6 of this chapter and in 18:3-5 among other passages. The many waters upon which she sits are interpreted explicitly (stated in vs. 15) as peoples and nations.

2. Her sin. 17:2.

2. Her dominant position over the nations could be political or spiritual. Those interpreters who believe the domination is political identify the harlot as the Roman Empire. Those expositors who consider the rule and subjugation are spiritual/religious, among who the present writer is one, identify her as papal Rome with the inclusion under her hegemony of all systems and sects which are basically antichristian, not excluding apostate Christendom. So grievous were her acts of immorality (mentioned twice in this verse) that the results are likened to a drunken stupor.

3. Her seat on the scarlet beast. 17:3.

3. In verse 1 the position of the harlot was described as to its wide scope, all nations and peoples; here she is seen sitting (dominating and domineering) on a scarlet beast. Is the harlot the same person as this woman? Context and logic demand an affirmative reply. The meaning of her riding the scarlet beast, replete with blasphemous names and having seven heads and ten horns, is that the

religious system is controlling and subjugating the political power. Cf. 13:1 for the connection with the beast from the sea. In short, at Rome the political power is under the absolute sway of the religious system. This was revealed supernaturally to John by the inditing Spirit. The scarlet color indicates the glory and splendor of the political power, but it cannot hinder the suppressive control of the religious leaders.

4. Her clothing. 17:4.

Some six elements are introduced to demonstrate the wealth, luxury, and extravagance of the harlot. But all is utilized to the one end — her uncleanness and immorality (cf. 18:9-19 for a picure of extensive wealth). The cup here is related to the enticements spoken of in verse 2.

5. Her name. 17:5.

5. There is no mistaking her identity, for her name is written on her forehead. Roman harlots in their brazenness wore a label with their names on their foreheads (cf. R. H. Charles, *op. cit.*, II, p. 65). The name contains a mystery, a disclosed secret for this time. Her widespread influence is underscored by the repeated references to her greatness. She is the source of godlessness and idolatrous practices throughout the world. (Cf. for a lengthy sketch, H.A. Ironside, *op. cit.*, pp. 285-302.) In the Greek text of the United Bible Societies her name is in normal lower case except for the B in "Babylon"; AV, ASV, NASB, and NIV use the upper case. What is the intended meaning of this verse? It is stating that literal Babylon of old is typical, symbolical of religious Babylon (cf. Jer 50:38; 51:7). For a parallel usage see 11:8 of Revelation. Mystery Babylon is in fact the mystery of iniquity in its final form (cf. II Thess 2:7).

6. Her bloodthirstiness. 17:6.

6. To this point one may feel that the harlot system is

guilty of atrocities in the moral and spiritual realms alone. But she is culpable of much more. The blood of saints and witnesses for Christ has stained her hands. In 18:24, the climax of the two chapters on Babylon, she is again charged with the blood of all God's prophets and saints who have been martyred on earth. Thus, the harlot cannot be literal Babylon nor papal Rome alone; it must comprehend all godless systems, consummating at last in this hideous figure. Here it is professing Christendom with her motley followers persecuting and slaying the saints of God; it is not now pagan emperors as in the days of the early Christian centuries. No wonder John was amazed. He was astonished that the professing church of his day could become so degenerate in a coming day.

7. The mystery of the woman. 17:7.

7. What the Apostle John saw still needed to be explained to him in its details. Since the disclosure was granted him, not to perplex him but to instruct him, the angel (cf. vs. 1) promises to clarify the mystery of both the woman and the beast.

8. Identity of the beast. 17:8-13.

8. There is a consensus of interpreters that the beast (the same as 13:1) is the Roman Empire: its historic appearance, its long disappearance, and its future reappearance. As to its motivation in reappearing, it will come from the abyss, devilish empowering, and finally find its end in perdition. The ancient Roman Empire in its imperial form in John's time was destroyed in A.D. 476. That political power has no present existence in the political world. But Satan will see that it is revived to fulfill his purpose. Notice that the beast as to his human origin is from the nations (cf. 13:10), but as to its supporting power it is a satanic revival. Such a resurrection of the old Roman Empire, almost endlessly scoffed at by unbelievers and even many believers, will amaze the

earth-dwellers, who are plainly stated to be unbelievers. John wondered (vs. 6); the world of a coming day will also wonder (vs. 9).

9. It is immediately stated that it takes God's wisdom to understand the disclosure. The seven mountains (or hills) are proof that mystical Babylon cannot be ancient literal Babylon, which was situated in a plain and not on mountains. However, it is known that Rome is built on seven hills (e.g., the Quirinal, Capitoline, Palatine); classical writers familiarly spoke of "the city of seven hills" (cf. Charles, *op. cit.*, II, p. 69).

10. If there has been a variety of views to this point, it has surely been increased to confusion in verses 10 and 11. Who are the seven kings? The text plainly states that five are past, one is present, and the last is future. R. H. Charles (*op. cit.*, II, p. 69; followed by Barclay, *op. cit.*, p. 181 *et al*) names them as Augustus, Tiberius, Caligula, Claudius, and Nero, then Vespasian, and finally Titus. The reign of the last is held to be a short one, thus fulfilling the text. However, much discussion has been expended on the state of the original manuscript and a Nero *redivivus* (resurrected) from 17:8, 11, 14. It is a poor exegesis to find fault with the condition of the original Greek when the interpretation does not fit the exigencies of the case. History will verify that in Roman rule six types of government are to be found: kings, consuls, dictators, decemvirs, and military tribunes; the sixth is the imperial form, which was in existence when John was on Patmos. The seventh type is the Roman Empire under a new head (cf. 13:1). His government will have ten kingdoms (cf. Dan 2 and 7), never equalled before and all subject to the beast (cf. Gaebelein, *in loco;* also Ottman, pp. 309-311). His tenure of office will be brief.

11. The human revival of the empire (cf. 13:1) in the Tribulation Period will be followed by the hellish revival

(cf. 17:8), which is so complete in itself as to be called an eighth feature (eight is the number of resurrection). There will be an organic connection between the last two stages of the Roman Beast in his sovereignty. He will be one of the seven, but distinct enough to be considered the eighth (cf. Dan 7:7, 8, 23-26).

12. The ten king kingdom (cf. 13:1) is the form in which the Roman Empire will be revived. It has never existed thus before (cf. Dan chs. 2 and 7). Verse 10 and 12 both stress the shortness of this rule: "a little while" and "for one hour." The precise time has been given earlier in the book more than once.

13. The confederated kings of the revived Roman Empire will have one mind and purpose: total subservience to the Roman Beast.

9. The victory of the Lamb. 17:14-18.

14. What is the goal of the confederated powers? Nothing less than war against the Lamb. Recall the war in heaven between Michael and his angels (cf. 12:7 ff.) and the dragon and his angels — quite an unequal combat. But here the balance of power is infinitely against the ungodly armies. The issue is never in doubt; it is victory for the Lamb and His redeemed (not angels) in heaven as can be discerned from the three adjectives that conclude the verse. Notice the honorific, well-deserved title of the Lamb. Here by anticipation is another preview of Armageddon, yet to be fully set forth in 19:14-21.

15. In an apocalyptic book with rich symbolism and a multiplicity of participants introduced in the narrative, there is need for occasional explanation, so this verse identifies the waters of verse 1.

16. Here illumination is given concerning the beast and his underlings who were dominated by the apostate system (vs. 3). In some way not stated, the subservient ones turn the tables and vent their hatred against the

harlot. So thoroughgoing will be their judgment on her, that it must be expressed by four concepts: desolation, nakedness, consumption (cannibalism), and burning. Cf. with the fate of Jezebel of old, II Kings 9:30-37.

17. Overruling all the feelings of the enemies of the harlot, it will ultimately be God who directs them to execute His judgment on her. All He has given in the prophetic word must be fulfilled.

18. The woman of this verse is the same as the one in verse 16 and indeed throughout the chapter. This verse is not an unnecessary addendum to the chapter. It reveals (1) that the woman (harlot), though a colossal system of apostasy and idolatry, is also to be thought of in terms of the city of her headquarters, namely, Rome; and (2) that her reign is worldwide. No wonder that when the head of the papal system addresses his followers, he does so by the salutation: "Urbi et orbi!" (To the city [that is, Rome] and the world!).

B. Fall of Babylon. Ch. 18.

This chapter carries on the subject of God's judgment on Babylon. Strangely enough, some writers have understood chapter 17 to speak of one person and system, and chapter 18 to deal with a totally different individual. The Scriptures use multiple figures, and the careful student will have sufficient clues to come to the proper understanding of each passage. Since the church is the Bride of Christ and a city, the New Jerusalem (cf. 21:9, 10), there is no valid reason to deny that Babylon is the harlot and a city (cf. 18:10). It is proper to think of Babylon in chapter 17 as a vast religious (ecclesiastical) system (cf. vss. 2, 4, 6), and also in chapter 18 as a huge interlocking commercial system (cf. vss. 3, 11-17). The present chapter pictures the doom of so-called Christian civilization in its social and commercial aspects. Civilization ever since the time of Cain has followed a path apart from God. See Genesis 4:16-24: cities, property, music, skilled art, polygamy, violence, and murder. (Cf. W. R. Newell, *op. cit.*, pp. 281-285, for his masterful treatment of "The Character of Commerce" and his inclusion of the equally able, extended quotation from J. A. Seiss, *The Apocalypse.*) Since the Hebrew ephah is emblematic of commerce, compare Zechariah 5:5-11 (esp. vs. 11: "in the land of Shinar") with the present chapter in the Revelation.

1. The glorious angel. 18:1.

1. Although this angel is introduced by the general word "another," he is not one connected with the bowls of wrath mentioned in 17:1. Two features indicate his importance: (1) great authority (there are degrees of authority among the angels), and (2) the ability to illuminate the earth with his glory. The strong probability is that Christ is meant here as in 8:3 and 10:1. In the first reference He is the Angel-Priest; in the second He is the Angel-Redeemer; here He is the Angel-Avenger of His own.

2. Babylon's fall realized. 18:2.

2. In 14:8 the announcement of the fall of Babylon was proleptic; similarly, in 16:19 the statement was brief and anticipatory. But here the purpose of God concerning her is actualized. True, in chapter 17 Babylon's doom is brought about by the ten kingdoms and the Roman Beast (the political power); here her downfall is seen as issuing directly from Christ. Surely, there is no discrepancy here, for 17:17 states clearly God's sovereign, righteous employment of the human factors in accomplishing His purpose. Just as idolatry came into the human sphere in Genesis 11 with Babylon of old (there is no record of idolatry before the flood of Noah), so it will have its hideous, unclean, hateful consummation in the Babylonish system of the future. All Satan's evil agencies will con-

gregate in her. There will be no freedom there, for "prison" is mentioned twice. It is a veritable cesspool of corruption.

3. Babylon's guilt. 18:3.

3. Again, the universality of her sway is underscored as in 17:1, 2, 15, 18. All the nations are pointed out here as the subjects of her deceptions and seductions. Godless religion knows how to capture the attention of the unwary world by display, ritual, and easy means of redemption, and vast amounts of wealth. The kings of the earth referred to now are not those included in the ten kingdom confederation; these are the ones outside that conglomerate. An additional element is introduced in the merchants (Gr *emporoi*, to which the Eng emporium is related) of the earth, and their riches and wealth are set forth (along with sensuality). There is a commercial side to Mystery Babylon.

4. Call to flee the doomed city. 18:4-8.

4, 5. The voice now is not that of the angel of verse 1. It is directed to God's people. Before judgment falls on the wicked (cf. Noah and his family, Gen 6:13-22; Lot and his daughters, Gen 19:12-22; and, as has been shown in this book, the church in the Rapture before the Tribulation Period, Rev 4:1 ff.), God mercifully warns His own in order to deliver them from the coming catastrophe. Thus, the call is applicable at all times as far as the apostate system is concerned. Cf. Hebrews 13:13. It will be all the more applicable in the time of the context of this chapter. In short, believing Jews and Gentiles will heed the warning and will escape the burning destruction.

Ancient, literal Babylon wanted to build a tower (ziggurat for their gods), as stated in Genesis 11:4. Here her mystical counterpart piled up her sins to heaven, an affront to the thrice holy God of heaven and earth. When it is indicated that God has remembered her iniquities, it is not that He had forgotten them previously. It is the biblical way of stating that the hour of reckoning and judgment had arrived.

6-8. Because Babylon's sins have accumulated over so long a period to time, and she has been impervious over the centuries to God's loving entreaties to repent, the Mosaic law of recompense in kind is doubled (cf. Ex 21:23-25). The summons in verses 6 and 7 could well be addressed to the church in the light of I Corinthians 6:2. The root of Babylon's degeneration was her pride, self-security, godlessness, and apotheosis of wealth and luxury, all directed toward self-glorification. The Lord God in His omnipotence will be her Judge (cf. Isa 47:9-11). The visitation is detailed in five particulars: plagues, pestilence, mourning, famine, and fire. All this will come upon her "in one day."

5. The mourning of kings and merchants. 18:9-20.

9, 10. In the verses under consideration (vss. 9-20) weeping and mourning are repeated as a theme in a sonata. First, the kings of the earth, who have the most to lose in any economic or commercial collapse, will lament inconsolably over the torment and demise of the wicked system, which has interlocking interests throughout the civilized world. They cry out woe upon the great and strong city, whose judgment has overtaken her. The "one day" of verse 8 is now "one hour," a clear indication that mathematical precision is not intended. It will be in a very short time. Fair weather friends that they are, the kings bewail Babylon's calamity, but stand at a distance lest they become involved in her misery and agony.

11-17a. The merchants, who are directly involved in day-by-day transactions with her, mourn over the economic collapse of that vast system with so many commercial ramifications. The cargoes include some twenty-eight distinct items. Here there is a combination of the religious with the commercial, for it begins with gold and ends with human lives (vs. 14). The list includes costly ornaments, costly raiment, costly furniture, costly perfumes, costly food, costly equipages, and men's souls and bodies (cf. W. Pettingill, *The Unveiling of Jesus Christ*, p. 80). The wealth of the world will be thrown into confusion and hopeless collapse.

17b-19. Moreover, the fall of commercial Babylon has serious consequences for maritime projects, involving shipmasters, sailors, and passengers. All will be crippled "in one hour" (cf. vss. 17, 19). The losses will be irretrievable.

20. What a change is now before the reader. The scene is shifted to heaven and God's perspective. The dwellers there — saints, apostles, and prophets, believers of every station — are summoned to rejoicing. Earth mourns but heaven rejoices (cf. 19:1-6). This reveals how out of tune with heaven earth dwellers can be. Saints, when in their pilgrimage on earth, suffered grievously at the hands of the apostate system, but now is the hour of their vindication, and they exult in God's justice.

6. The finality of her doom. 18:21-23.

21-23. Her ruin is final, complete, and irreversible. The symbolism in verse 21 is related to Jeremiah 51:63, 64, which bears out the impossibility of recovery from this judgment. Along with the passing of the city, there will be an end of music, crafts, housekeeping ("sounds of a mill"), illumination, and the joys of marriage. The cause of it all is her deception of all the nations with her religious sorcery, an activity promoted by demons and Satan. Included is the entire system of ungodliness from the beginning of man's sojourn on earth.

7. The reason for her fall. 18:24.

24. Any pity or compassion on her is misspent and misdirected, for she is worthy of all the misery and judg-

ment God pours out on her. She is guilty of the blood of martyred prophets and saints who were ever slain on the earth. This inclusive statement shows that more than one apostate organization is meant; it involves the totality of them all from man's appearance on earth until the coming of the Son of man to earth.

13 The Supper of the Lamb and the Supper of God

Chapter 19

Here are recorded the events toward which the Book of Revelation has steadily been leading. Until the usurper on earth (the harlot) is judged, the bride (the church) is not made manifest. The harlot and the bride do not occupy the scene of action at the same time.

A. Hallelujahs in Heaven, 19:1-6.

1, 2. It is after the doom of mystical Babylon ("after these things" — see the same Gr wording in 4:1), fully detailed in chapters 17 and 18, that the invitation to rejoice in 18:20 can be fulfilled. Those participating are indicated only as a great multitude (cf. also vs. 6). There is not profit in seeking to particularize here, when the designation is so broad. It is all the redeemed in heaven including the twenty-four elders and the four living creatures (vs. 4). The rejoicing begins with the word "Hallelujah," which occurs four times in this chapter (vss. 1, 3, 4, 6). It is a transliterated (not translated) Hebrew word, found no other place in the New Testament. In fact, even in the Old Testament, especially in the Book of Psalms, it is correctly translated "Praise the Lord!" It is thus interesting that four times in the Revelation the Hebrew word (actually two words) should be found. It is indeed a beautiful word known worldwide, which needs no translation. Augustine said that the feeling and saying of the word incorporate all the blessedness of heaven (cf. J. A. Seiss, *in loco*). Earth knows much of blasphemy and vile vituperation against God and His blessed Name, but heaven gloriously rings with His praises. Three attributes of God are singled out for acclamation: salvation, glory, and power. W. Barclay has well stated: "Each of these three great attributes of God should awaken its own response in the heart of man, and these responses taken together constitute real praise. The *salvation* of God should awaken the *gratitude* of man. The *glory* of God should awaken the *reverence* of man. The *power* of God is always exercised in the love of God, and should, therefore, awaken the *trust* of man. Gratitude, reverence, trust — these are the constituent elements of real praise" (*op. cit.*, II, p. 218).

The attributes of truth and righteousness have been clearly witnessed in the judgment of the great harlot. The latter part of verse 2 could well apply to the martyrs, though the language is couched in the third person.

3. Apparently, the same company utter the second Hallelujah. They give praise for the finality, the completeness, and eternal character of Babylon's judgment.

4. The reader is here immediately reminded of those who worship and praise God in chapter 4. They join the heavenly Hallelujah Chorus.

5. With so much praise and adoration filling the scene, one would not expect further summons to praise and extol God. But even after the third Hallelujah, it must be stressed that God is worthy of nothing less than eternal praise. All God's bondservants of whatever rank or position are included in the invitation to praise Him, for the word of invitation comes from the seat of God's government.

6. With this verse there appears to be a crescendo reached, as the wording indicates. Handel in his oratorio of "The Messiah" has correctly caught the climax: "Hallelujah! For the Lord our God, the Almighty, reigns."

This is the hour for which the church has prayed and longed, and all creation has groaned (cf. Rom 8:18-23). Before Christ assumes His rightful throne on earth, Babylon must be judged on earth, and His marriage celebrated in heaven. The first is past (chs. 17, 18); the second follows here. What was stated by way of anticipation in 11:15 is now realized.

B. The Marriage of the Lamb. 19:7-10.

7-10. Of all the provisions of God for man's well-being and joy on earth, marriage, God's first social institution, ranks second only to that of salvation. Both Old and New Testament give ample evidence of the importance of this symbolism. Hosea spoke of it from a traumatic experience in his own life (cf. Hos 2:19, 20); Isaiah spoke glowingly of it (cf. Isa 54:5); Jeremiah dwelt on the theme (cf. Jer 3:14; 31:31, 32); and Ezekiel portrayed it with fulness (cf. Ezk 16). The New Testament speaks of the marriage feast (cf. Mt 22:2), the bridal chamber and the wedding garment (cf. Mt 22:10, 11), the sons of the bridal chamber (cf. Mk 2:19), the bridegroom (cf. Mt 25:1; Mk 2:19), and the friends of the bridegroom (cf. Jn 3:29). Paul writes of the church as the betrothed virgin of Christ (cf. II Cor 11:2), and of the pattern of the relationship between husband and wife (cf. Eph 5:21-33). Cf. Barclay, *The Revelation of John*, pp. 222-23.

7. The wording of verse 7 is unusual and must not be overlooked. In normal parlance the wedding is spoken of as the marriage of the bride, but here it is "the marriage of the Lamb." And rightly so, for the chief joy is His. It takes place in heaven, and no details are given. Care is to be exercised in speaking of the relationship of Israel and the church with reference to marriage, so that biblical norms are not violated. Israel is the unfaithful, yet to be reclaimed, wife of the Lord in the Old Testament; the church is the bride of Christ the Lamb in the New Testa-

ment. Once the wife or bride is mentioned, there is no further reference in the book to elders as in verse 4.

8. For this glorious occasion the bride of necessity had to make herself ready. The preparation includes: (1) acceptance of the marriage offer of the Lamb, which is regeneration; (2) the desire to be properly clothed for the wedding; (3) a willingness to receive what is given her for the joyous event. When the bride clothes herself, it is with the finest of apparel. Her basic clothing is the garment of salvation, which she received at her acceptance of the Lamb's gracious offer of marriage (cf. Isa 61:10). Now in addition to the initial clothing she has *given* to her (still all of grace) bright, clean fine linen. It is identified as the righteous acts (Gr is plural, *dikaiomata*) of the saints. How has she obtained these? It is inescapable that the judgment seat of Christ has already been held in order to grant rewards to the saints for faithful service to Christ (cf. II Cor 5:10). What a recognition day that will be!

9. But another important element of every wedding is the guests, so John is instructed to indicate the blessedness of those invited to the marriage supper of the Lamb. These are the friends of the Bridegroom (cf. Jn 3:29); the guests are seen in another figure as the virgins, the companions of the bride (cf. Ps 45:9, 14). They are probably all Old Testament saints. All others than the church are the guests at the marriage supper. Lest some reader consider these words to be too good to be true, the mediating angel (cf. 1:1) informs the apostle that the words are sure and certain, because they come from God.

10. The disclosure of truth was so marvelous and perhaps the appearance of the angel was so striking, that John was moved to worship at his feet. When John did this at Christ's feet (cf. 1:17), he received no rebuke, but was rather delivered from fear. But in 19:10 and 22:8, 9, the apostle is forbidden such worship, for no creature in

heaven, on earth, or under the earth is permitted to receive man's worship. Men may receive honor and respect (cf. Rom 12:10; 13:7), but no creature may receive worship. Angels are servants on the basis of creation; believers are servants on the basis of redemption. All homage and worship belong to Jesus to whom all prophecy points. The last sentence in verse 10 is one of the most important in all Scripture. Plainly stated, it declares that the witness and testimony that are borne to Jesus, are the motivating and underlying purpose of all prophecy. Prophecy is meant to convey an indispensable witness to Jesus.

C. The Visible Coming of Christ. 19:11-16.

11. Now heaven is opened to the gaze of John; he had seen it open several times before (cf. 4:1 *et al*), but never on such a sight as this. Cf. Acts 1:11; esp. Rev. 1:7. Here John sees the One with dyed garments from Bozrah of Isaiah's prophecy, the righteous Branch and King of Jeremiah's prediction, the returning Shekinah glory of Ezekiel's foretelling, the Stone cut out without hands of Daniel's announcement, the Lord coming with His saints of Zechariah's prophecy, and the appearing of the Son of man of the Saviour's own prophecy. Cf. Matthew 24:29, 30. The white horse symbolizes victory and triumph. He is faithful and true in His character and every deed. Indeed, He is the mighty Warrior who will right the world's every ill (cf. Acts 17:31). He judges and wars under the same principle, that is, righteousness.

12. The description of His glorious Person continues. His eyes indicate penetrating, scrutinizing omniscience. On that blessed head, once crowned at Calvary for sinful man, rest many diadems. His is supreme authority. Saints have crowns; He has diadems. The Roman beast (cf. 13:1) has diadems also, but only because he assumes absolute

authority. But how can one head have many diadems? They are in tiers one above another, indicating highest majesty and authority. Many things have been divulged in the Apocalypse so far, and more will follow to the end of the book, but there are certain elements which must remain hidden from man (cf. Deut 29:29). From scriptural usage it is known that the name indicates His own essential glory, which expresses the fullness of His divine nature.

13. The Redeemer does not come now to save, but to judge. The robe dipped in blood points to the activity in Isaiah 63:1-6 (see vs. 15). The judgment of Christ will be exercised to the fullest. His Name, the Word of God, shows that He is the full expression (as a word is of the thought in the mind) of God, now in judgment (cf. II Thess 1:7-10).

14. Who are the armies in fine white linen on white horses? Good men differ as to their identity. All are agreed that they are believers, redeemed ones; some even include the angels. It appears that they are, first, the church, second, the Tribulation saints, then the Old Testament saints. Jude 14, 15 will then be fulfilled.

15. The description continues, not merely to fill out the portrait, but to reveal the activity with which the Lord of glory is occupied. The sharp sword issuing from His mouth is undoubtedly the Word of God (cf. Isa 11:4; Heb 4:12), but specifically in judgment. The nations, the objects of His rule, will be ruled with a rod of iron (cf. Ps 2:9; Rev 12:5). Stern and inflexible, but always absolutely righteous, will the rule be. He has ample power to implement His every command. Besides the mention of sword and rod of iron, there is now the figure of the winepress. Again, this is the figure of the vintage (cf. Isa 63:1-6; Rev 14:19, 20).

16. In addition to the two names connected with the

returning Lord Jesus (cf. vss. 12, 13), there is another on His robe and thigh. It has been introduced already in 17:14 but in reverse order. It is His full majestic name in His glorious position relative to the earth, visible for all to read. Such a title was arrogantly assumed by men in the ancient Near East. Conquering kings allowed their subjugated, royal enemies to retain their former title in order to convey the idea that they, the victorious ones, were the highest and supreme above all. To be sure, this was empty boasting, but not with the conquering Christ.

D. The Supper of God: Armageddon. 19:17-19.

17. Actually, the picture of Armageddon continues on through verse 21, but the account narrows down in verses 20 and 21 to the two principal offenders of the time, the beast and the false prophet. Although the record is not an extended one, it is the last treatment of the subject of Armageddon, the former two references (cf. 14:18-20 and 16:13-16) being anticipatory and on the whole general. One must not expect a recital of a war such as is found in extra-biblical works, because the objective in Scripture is quite different. The details of the war are given under the figure of a supper in contrast to the marriage supper of the Lamb. The invitation is addressed to all the birds who fly in midheaven. The vultures remind of Matthew 24:27, 28, as well as Isaiah 34:2-6.

18. Notice the inclusiveness of those who are involved in the conflict: kings, commanders (captains), mighty men, horses, their riders, all men, free and slaves, small and great. Five times the word "flesh" is found in this verse; a vast feast of carrion is envisaged. No wonder, for it takes place on an ideal battlefield, the most famous in the world. Among the battles fought there are: Sisera against Barak (cf. Jud 5:19); Gideon against the Mi-

dianites (cf. Jud 6:33); Saul and Jonathan against the Philistines (cf. I Sam 31); King Josiah against Pharaoh Necho (cf. II Kgs 23:20); on the western border Elijah contended with the prophets of Baal (I Kgs 18:39); Ahaziah died there (cf. II Kgs 9:27). It has been the scene of conflict from ancient times to modern days. The Scripture passages, which are relevant, are Psalm 2:1-3; Ezekiel 38 and 39; Joel 3:9-16; Zechariah 12:1-9; 14:1-4, besides others in the Old and New Testament. In the Revelation, 9:13-18; 14:14-20; and 16:12-14, 16, have already prepared the way for the final treatment in this chapter. In view of the foregoing comments it is difficult to understand how an able scholar can state: "Since Megiddo is not associated with any eschatological expectation, it is possible some corruption underlies this word" (cf. R. H. Charles, *op. cit.*, II, p. 50). Another writer feels that "such a Mount does not appear elsewhere in Scripture or in other ancient literature" (cf. R. C. H. Lenski, *op. cit.*, p. 479). Yet another comments: "Har-Magedon is the symbol of every battle in which, when the need is greatest and believers are oppressed, the Lord reveals his power in the interest of his distressed people and defeats the enemy" (cf. W. Hendriksen, *op. cit.*, p. 196). To such extremes are some men driven when they forsake the literal interpretation of prophecy.

19. The Roman political leader (cf. 13:1) musters his following among the kings of the earth with their respective armies to do battle with Christ and His followers (cf. vss. 14, 15). There will be no need for the redeemed to fight. The encounter will be both short and decisive.

E. Judgment of the Beast and False Prophet. 19:20,21.

20, 21. Now the chief antagonists, the beast (cf. 13:1) and the false prophet (cf. 13:11), are seized and thrown alive into the lake of fire. The false prophet (the Antichrist, religious leader) is singled out, because it was he who worked miracles to seduce and deceive men (cf. II Thess 2:1-12). It is remarkable that these two ungodly leaders find their final place of judgment even before Satan does (cf. 20:7-10). Their followers are slain by the sword of Christ; notice the wording of II Thessalonians 2:8: ". . . the Lord will slay with the breath of His mouth" to learn the literalness of these events. The final word is that the supper of God filled the appetite of all the birds. Horrendous carnage it will be.

14 The Millennial Reign of Christ

Chapter 20

This chapter is a Continental Divide of Scripture. If one follows a single, consistent hermeneutical principle in Scripture interpretation, it will lead him to one perspective on this chapter. If, on the other hand, one should employ a dual hermeneutic (one for non-prophetic portions of Scripture and another for the prophetic parts), it will carry him to a totally different interpretation of this pivotal chapter. Premillennialists (also known as chiliasts from the Greek word for 1,000) use a single interpretive principle and find in this vital chapter that, after the visible coming of Christ in chapter 19, He will set up His earthly kingdom and reign with His saints for a thousand years, while Satan (the Roman Beast and the Antichrist have already been cast into the lake of fire) is confined to the abyss. Later the evil trio are found in the lake of fire to remain there forever. Amillennialists employ a dual hermeneutic in interpretation and find no earthly reign of Christ either predicted in the Old or New Testament or realized in a thousand year kingdom. For them Satan was bound by Christ (contra I Pet 5:8) and is in such imprisonment throughout the church age. As to the two resurrections of chapter 20, one is said to be spiritual and the other literal and final. The student will do well to consult the bibliography at the end of this commentary for those of one persuasion or the other. There is an admission on the part of some that in the Early Church the millennial view was dominant, if not general, because of the Jewish view of the Messianic rule of the Son of God, fortified, they say, by the teaching of the apocalyptic works which arose between the Old and New Testament. But when Christian doctrine became more explicit, chiliasm was rejected. The fact is that chiliasm was dominant until Augustine rebelled against it and introduced his spiritualizing method of interpreting prophecy. For a full discussion of the question, see the present writer's *Millennialism: The Two Major Views*, Moody Press, 1980 and 1982.

A. The Binding of Satan. 20:1 3.

1-3. This chapter follows the events of the previous chapter. Satan has been on earth since 12:9, carrying on his blighting work though unseen by mortal eye. The angel is probably the Lord Jesus Christ, for He alone is a match for Satan (Michael is not, cf. Jude 9). The scene is admittedly symbolic (cf. 1:1), because a spirit being is not susceptible to treatment by keys and chains. The key is to lock and the chain is to bind. In the last analysis, God has authority over the abyss.

The purpose of the angel is to bind Satan for a thousand years. Dragon indicates cruelty; serpent speaks of guile; devil indicates him as the tempter of man; and Satan indicates he is the adversary of Christ and His people. From verse 2 through 7 there are six mentions of 1,000 years. If this number is symbolic, of what is it a symbol? It cannot mean that which is endless, because the Greek language, as well as the Hebrew, has ample means to convey the thought without ambiguity.

Thrown into the abyss, Satan is incarcerated, so that he is unable to deceive the nations for the length of that period, namely, the Millennium. The sealing is for security, as elsewhere in Scripture. He is adequately curbed and restrained. What a boon to mankind is this! Deception has characterized Satan from Genesis 3 to the time now under consideration. Cf. II Corinthians 4:3, 4. In God's purpose Satan will be loosed after the allotted time. Why? Simply, God would reveal to us that he has not changed his nature, and that man still is susceptible to his wiles and stratagems. The result of the loosing is indicated in verses 7 and 8.

B. The Resurrection and Reign of the Saints. 20:4-6.

4. What was seen in 11:15 by way of anticipation is here realized. It is understood that Christ will sit on His throne and reign as the legitimate Son of David, and it is clearly stated in the last clauses of this verse. Who are the occupants of the thrones? From the combined testimony of Scripture they will be New Testament saints (cf. I Cor 6:2), who reign as the Queen of the King. Too, there will be Old Testament saints, who will rule as vicegerents of the King and Queen (cf. Deut 28:1, 13; Mt 19:28). The martyred through the Tribulation Period, and those who resisted the idol worship of the beast, will also reign. These will come to life (only a literal, not spiritual resurrection, will meet the demands of the context where individuals have been beheaded) and reign with Christ for the Millennium.

5. The rest of the dead do not experience resurrection until the 1,000 years have run their course. Thus it is pointless and baseless to speak of a general resurrection in order to avoid the intervening period of 1,000 years, as amillennialists do. The order of the resurrection can be gleaned from these Scriptures: I Corinthians 15:23, 24; Revelation 20:4-6; Daniel 12:1-3; and Luke 20:34-36. The word "first" is found in verses 5 and 6. Words are emptied of meaning if this means there is but one resurrec-

tion. There are definite stages in the first resurrection, the chief one is Christ Himself (cf. I Cor 15:20).

6. Blessed and holy are all who have part in the first resurrection, i.e., of the righteous. "Blessed" tells of their condition; "holy" speaks of their character. They are priests and kings (cf. 1:6; I Peter 2:5), exactly as Christ combines the two offices (cf. Zech 6:13). The reign with Christ, prophesied in Old and New Testament alike, will endure for 1,000 years. Over these righteous ones the second death (the lake of fire, vs. 14) has no sway; it holds no terror for them through the all-sufficient work of the Saviour.

C. The Final Doom of Satan, the Beast, and the False Prophet. 20:7-10.

7. After the Millennium Satan is released from his imprisonment in the abyss. It is for the last exhibition of his venom and the last test of man.

8. After Christ's glorious mediatorial reign on earth for 1,000 years, Satan stages a rebellion through his deceptions. Notice, first of all, it is on a universal scale, namely, the nations. How could this occur? It must be remembered that there will be procreation in the Millennium on the part of those who have entered the kingdom (cf. Mt 25:31-46) in unresurrected bodies, but their progeny will not be born redeemed any more than this has transpired at any time in the history of man. Cf. Isaiah 65:20. Furthermore, many will give only feigned obedience to the ruling King (cf. Ps 66:3 in the NASB).

Are the Gog and Magog here the same as those of Ezekiel 38, 39? Definitely not, for four reasons: (1) the chronological factor. The events of Ezekiel 38, 39 take place before the Millennium in Israel's latter days (cf. the present writer's *The Book of Ezekiel*, Moody Press, 11th printing, 1982, pp. 218-239). The rebellion of Revelation 20 occurs after the Millennium. (2) The geographical factor. More than once Ezekiel clearly states that Gog and Magog come from the uttermost parts of the north of the land of promise. Here John explicitly locates the nations involved as coming from the four corners of the earth. (3) The actuating factor. It is true that Satan can be faulted for much of the ungodliness in the world, but there are also the elements of the flesh and the world (cf. Eph 2:1-3). It cannot be denied that Satan is behind the invasion of Ezekiel 38, 39, but not in so clearly a stated manner as here. (4) The interpretive factor. The reader of the Apocalypse will certainly assent by this time that John uses common nouns, and even proper nouns, in a symbolic manner. Witness the use of Jezebel (cf. 2:20), Sodom and Egypt (cf. 11:8), and Babylon (cf. the most extended use of symbolism in a name in chs. 17 and 18). Thus the student of the Revelation need not be surprised to find the names Gog and Magog used symbolically here. Cf. W. F. Arndt and F. W. Gingrich, *A Greek-English Lexicon of the New Testament*, p. 167, col. 2. Sad, indeed, it is that after such a benevolent and beneficent rule of the Lord of glory, there should be a following of Satan like the sand of the sea.

9. These nations will be banded together for one purpose and will press on toward one goal, namely, to destroy the capital city of the king, Jerusalem, and work havoc among His faithful subjects. God delights in Jerusalem and calls it "the beloved city," because outside its walls the Son of God accomplished redemption for the world in the will of the Father, and then has reigned in righteousness in that city for 1,000 years. The judgment of God with fire on the invaders is swift and final.

10. Now the instigator to sin ever since the Garden of Eden is dealt with. His final doom is the lake of fire — unthinkable torment. It will be eternal and irreversible,

because the beast and false prophet, who were cast into
the lake of fire before the Millennium, are still there.
They will be preserved in judgment, not annihilated.
There will be never-ending mental agony and physical
suffering. Unbelievers scoff at the concept of anyone or
anything being preserved in fire. The same God, who
placed consuming power in fire, can, if He wills,
counteract that power. He has done so in the past (cf. the
Hebrew youths in the fiery furnace, Dan 3:27) and will in
the future (cf. Mk 9:49). If the torment is forever, why are
day and night introduced here? There will be no day or
night in eternity according to our chronological reckoning, but this is the clearest way to convey it to our minds,
which are accustomed to concepts of time and space.

D. The Great White Throne Judgment. 20:11-15.

Our amillennialist brethren, who are operating on a
unitary principle of one covenant, one people of God, one
resurrection, and one judgment, carry through this
hermeneutic here also. For them there will be the coming
of Christ, a general resurrection, and a general judgment.
Actually, the biblical doctrine of judgment is not so
simplistic, if all the scriptural data are taken into account.
True, the judgment in these verses is the final one, but it
is *not* the only one. The Bible reveals seven distinct
judgments: one past, one present, and five future.
Because of the tyranny of time and space, the first six will
be dealt with briefly, and the last one more fully. First,
there is the judgment of the Cross. It was a judgment in
two senses: (1) man's sins were judged at Calvary (cf. II
Cor 5:21; Gal 3:13; Rom 8:1), and (2) Satan was judged
there also (cf. Col 2:14, 15 with Jn 16:11). It is a judgment
past and never to be repeated. Second, there is the judgment of the sinning believer (cf. I Cor 11:30-32), if he does
not judge himself. The more often this judgment is ex-

perienced, the better. Third is the judgment of the
believer's works (cf. Rom 14:10; I Cor 3:10-19; 4:5; II Cor
5:10; Rev 22:12). This takes place at the Rapture (cf. II
Tim 4:8) at the judgment seat (*bēma*) of Christ in heaven.
It is for rewards or suffering loss (cf. I Cor. 3:14, 15).
Fourth, there is the judgment upon Israel (cf. Ezk
20:33-38; Mt 24:9, 10). It takes place after the Tribulation
Period; those who continue to reject their Messiah will
not enter the kingdom; those who have received Him will
enter (cf. Rom 11:26). Fifth, there will be a judgment of
the nations (cf. Joel 3:11-16; Mt 25:31-46). It will occur
after the Tribulation Period; it will be on the basis, as
always, of acceptance or rejection of Christ, manifested in
their treatment of the earthly brethren of our Lord. The
righteous enter the kingdom and eternal life; the wicked
are excluded from both. Sixth, this judgment will come
upon fallen angels and Satan (cf. II Pet 2:4; Jude 6; Rev
20:10). Time and place are not specified for the angels; the
beast and false prophet will be judged before the reign of
Christ, and Satan after the 1,000 years. Because of their
relentless rebellion against God, they will suffer eternal
fire. Seventh, this is the judgment now under consideration in Revelation 20:11-15. It is properly called The Great
White Throne Judgment.

11. This is the judgment of the wicked dead, distinct
from all the previous ones just considered. It is described
as "great," because it is the most awesome assize ever
held. The characterization "white" has reference to the
purity and holiness with which all will be conducted. The
"throne" indicates that there is majesty with authority
involved. The One who sits on the throne is the Lord
Jesus Christ (cf. Jn 5:22, 27; II Tim 4:1). To underscore the
gravity of the proceedings John states that heaven and
earth fled from His presence, and no place was found for
them. This does not mean the annihilation of the earth

and heaven. It is rather that, between the passing of the millennial scene and the entrance on the new heaven and earth, the Great White Throne Judgment will take place.

12. Where will the subjects of the judgment stand? They will be upheld by God in space. This is a deeply solemn scene which merges into eternity. The judgment is final and eternal, for all that are circumscribed, that is, earth and heaven, have passed away. The high and low of rank on earth will be there. The sinner is now brought face to face with God the Son, from whom he cannot escape. This verse is vital in its distinctions: notice that there are books and another book. Could not the latter be included in the former? By no means, because both entities are defined. The book is the book of life, in which are inscribed all who have trusted Christ. Here it is introduced to show that the subjects of the judgment are unsaved. The books contain the record of their deeds (cf. vss. 12, 13). Why is there need to consult their deeds, if they are lost? It is intended to reveal the number and gravity of their sins for degrees of punishment (cf. carefully Lk 12:47, 48).

13. Even the unsaved who have died on the seas, whose bodies have never been recovered, will not be exempt from this august tribunal (cf. Jn 5:28, 29). Death (used here for the grave) gives up the bodies; Hades gives up the souls. No one is said to escape or enter eternal bliss. All are unsaved and will suffer their eternal doom (cf. 20:6).

14. Death and Hades, brought into existence by man's sin, end where all sinners do, namely, the lake of fire. This means an actual, eternal separation from God in conscious, unceasing torment.

15. There is no indication that any individual at the Great White Throne ever escapes judgment. The cause of

their final doom — not that they did not accumulate sufficient good deeds in the books — is that their names were
not found written in the Lamb's book of life (cf. 3:5; 13:8;
21:27). This is all-inclusive from Cain to the end of human
history.

15 The New Heaven and Earth

Chapter 21

A. Passing of old heaven and earth. 21:1.

1. Prophecy does not deal at length with the eternal state; therefore, it is difficult for any man to answer the many questions posed by those who long for details. Even Paul, who was caught up to the third heaven which is the throne of God, was not permitted to divulge what he saw and heard (cf. II Cor 12:3, 4). Prophecy carries the reader to the end of the Millennium. References to the eternal state are few: Isaiah 65:17; 66:22; I Corinthians 15:24-28; Ephesians 3:21; and II Peter 3:13, together with the disclosures in Revelation 21 and 22.

Verse 1 of this chapter is to be connected with 20:11 (cf. II Peter 3:13). Scripture does not teach the annihilation of the material universe. God annihilates nothing, let alone human beings, as some erroneously teach. Earth and heaven will be completely purified. During the Millennium the earth is renovated (cf. Isa 35:1 ff.; Mt 19:28 ["regeneration" in this text has nothing to do with spiritual matters, but with the renovation of the earth]). Apparently, the new heaven will be the home of believers of this age; the new earth will be the residence of redeemed ones apart from the church. It is not to be expected that believers in these areas will not have constant communication and communion with each other. Both will be populated with redeemed, cleansed souls. Righteousness suffers now (the godly suffer, cf. II Tim 3:12); in the Millennium it will reign (cf. Isa 11:9; 32:1); in the eternal state it will dwell (cf. II Pet 3:13). John indicates that there will be no sea. This will give so much more land space in the eternal earth for the peoples on earth.

B. New Jerusalem. 21:2-7.

2. In popular thinking all mentions of Jerusalem in the Bible are referring to the same city. This is not true. Multiplied references in Scripture do speak of the literal, earthly city, the one David made his capital. But there are other references which do not have that city in view at all. How is one to distinguish in these cases? The Spirit of God, Master of language that He is, gives the student definite clues. For instance, in Galatians 4 Paul writes of "the present Jerusalem" (cf. vs. 25) and "the Jerusalem above" (cf. vs. 26). He is not speaking of cities at all; symbolically, he is contrasting the principles of law and grace. The writer of the Epistle to the Hebrews speaks of Abraham's looking for a city, whose architect is God (cf. 11:10, 16); then there is mention (cf. 12:22) of "the heavenly Jerusalem," which is doubtless the one of Revelation 21:2, which will be shown below. There is a millennial Jerusalem predicted in Isaiah 2:1-4, to which all the nations will flow, a true confluence of peoples. But there is yet another Jerusalem designated as the "New Jerusalem," with the added description that it is the holy city. Popular opinion equates the New Jerusalem with heaven; this is an error. The New Jerusalem comes down from heaven from God; even more, the city is called (vss. 9, 10) "the bride, the wife of the Lamb." Why? Because she is its most prominent inhabitant. Thus it is clear that, when other than the literal city is intended, the Spirit adds qualifying and descriptive words to make this known. Recall that Babylon will be both a harlot (cf. ch.

17) and a city (cf. ch. 18). Apparently, the descent of the city in verse 10 is at the beginning of the Millennium; the coming down in verse 2 is at the end of the Millennium into the eternal state. The church will be seen as an adorned bride throughout all eternity. The picture stresses the positional, because the New Jerusalem, somewhat in the way of a midway house, will be the meeting place of all the redeemed, as the city is suspended, from all appearances, above the millennial Jerusalem.

3. God dwelling among men, this was the purpose of the tabernacle of old (cf. Ex 25:8); indeed, it was the object of the incarnation (cf. Jn 1:14), Immanuel (God with us) in the most universal and complete sense (cf. Rev 7:15). A tabernacle suggests moving about; the saints will have access to all parts of God's creation. Undoubtedly, there will be communication between the earthly, millennial Jerusalem and the mystical or New Jerusalem. God will dwell with men; there will be no change in the eternal state.

4. All sin's effects will be done away with (cf. 7:17). The eye, called "the fountain of sorrow," will be dry, and that forever.

5. The One on the throne is the Father, for the kingdom has been delivered over to Him by the Son, the Mediator (cf. I Cor 15:24-28).

6. God is indeed the source and end of all glory (cf. Rom 11:36). He is the First (Alpha) and the Last (Omega). After their sin in Eden, Adam and Eve were prohibited from taking of the tree of life; here all are invited freely to take of the water of life through the redemption of Christ. No one will thirst in eternity, since Christ thirsted on Calvary when dying for us. It is still a valid offer from God now.

7. The overcomer here , as in chapters 2 and 3, is the believer, the one who has drunk of the water of life. For

him there is sonship with God forever.

C. The portion of the ungodly. 21:8.

    8. For the unrepentant, who are designated under some eight categories, there will be not bliss but burning in the lake of fire, the second death (cf. 20:6,14). A believer may be called on to pass through one death, i.e., physical death (and if the Rapture intervenes, he will forego that death, cf. I Cor 15:51, 52); an unbeliever faces two deaths: physical and the second death. Why are the cowardly and liars in the categories? The first are afraid to accept Christ and bear the ridicule of the world. The second are those who have denied their sin and need of Christ as Saviour.

D. The wife of the Lamb. 21:9.

    9. It is gracious of God to allow one of the angels who was commissioned to pour out the most horrendous plagues earth has ever known, the privilege of inviting John to a special view of the bride, the wife of the Lamb. For the remainder of the chapter there will be presented a symbolic description of the bride in all her millennial glory. Her relationship to Christ continues on into the eternal ages. Because the millennial picture approximates heaven, many have equated them. This is an error, for there are some in the Millennium, whose hearts have not been touched for God, who will enlist under Satan's banner in his rebellion against Christ (cf. 20:8, 9) at the end of that glorious reign. Amillennialists see this age of grace merging at the coming of Christ into the age of glory. Premillennialists believe that the age of grace will be followed by the age of righteousness (where Christ will be vindicated in time as He was rejected in history), which will then merge into the age of glory.

E. Description of the New Jerusalem. 21:10-27.

1. Its origin. 21:10.

10. Mark that John is transported by the Spirit to a vantage point where he can see the holy city, Jerusalem, in all her beauty and glory. Wonderful it is to read of Jerusalem as a holy city; the prophets inveighed against her in centuries past, because she was just the opposite (cf. Isa 1:4, 15, 18, 21; 5:7). It is unmistakably stated that this city proceeds from the heavenly realm; it is out of heaven. However, it is not to be equated with heaven, as indicated above.

2. Its brilliance. 21:11.

11. The description is given under the figure of precious stones, because (1) they are costly, and (2) they are durable. The Spirit uses language best adapted to our limited comprehension. The city will be brilliant and glorious.

3. Its wall. 21:12.

12. The wall indicates all will be secure within the city, and it will be separate from all that is unlike it in holiness. Notice that the foundation of the church was laid in Israel.

4. Its gates. 21:13.

13. Gates were places of judgment. Here is the fulfillment of Matthew 19:28.

5. Its foundation stones. 21:14.

14. The world may forget, and has, that it was the twelve apostles who laid the foundation for the church upon the foundation Stone, Christ Himself (cf. Eph 2:20). But God never forgets.

6. Its measurements. 21:15-17.

15-17. From the measurements given it is clear that the city is a cube 1,500 miles in each way.

7. Its materials. 21:18-21.

18-21. The gold (cf. vss. 18, 21) speaks, as in the tabernacle of old where the cherubim of gold were called the

cherubim of glory, of divine glory. All the stones named
are known for their value and beauty and enduring quality.

8. Its temple. 21:22.

22. Contrary to the long history of temples in Israel,
there will be no temple in the New Jerusalem. Does this
indicate an element of secularism? God forbid. Rather, it
means there will be free access to God; it will be for all
(recall that only priests could enter the sanctuary proper
and that only the High Priest could enter the Holy of
Holies, and that on one day a year). It will be immediate
access, and it will be without barrier (witness the calamity that befell Uzziah of Judah when he tried to offer incense in the holy place). Cf. II Chronicles 26:16-21.

9. Its illumination. 21:23.

23. God the Father and the Lamb will be the all-
sufficient light for the city. Therefore, there will be no
need of sun, moon, or lamp; the Lamb will meet every re-
quirement. Remember that in the temple, as in the tabernacle, there were three means of illumination. For the
outer court the illumination of the sun by day and the
moon by night were ample. For the inner sanctuary the
lampstand lighted all the furniture, because the light of
sun and moon did not penetrate there. For the Holy of
Holies the Shekinah provided all; this typified the blessed
light of the Lamb (cf. Jn 1:4, 9; 9:5).

10. The presence of the nations and their kings. 21:24.

24. The New Jerusalem with the church will be the
center of the governments of the earth. There has never
been a rule like it.

11. Continuous access. 21:25.

25. There will be unhindered access and no setting
sun, but full noon always. Ever since Adam and Eve
sinned, there has been a barrier to access. They could no
longer enjoy the Garden of Eden. Even Adam feared com-

munication with God and hid himself. When Israel accepted the yoke of the law (cf. Ex 19), immediately they were not allowed access to Mount Sinai on pain of death. When the tabernacle, and later the temple also, were constructed, God placed the symbol of His presence (the Shekinah, literally, the Dwelling-Presence of God) in the innermost compartment, as far from sinful man as possible, unless he came through his representative, the High Priest, with the blood of an offering. Now, in the New Jerusalem all blockades to access are removed and that forever.

12. The glory and honor of the nations. 21:26.

26. This verse builds on the truth of verse 24. But notice the glory of it. In the worship of Israel no Gentile could enter into the holy precincts without serious repercussions. Remember the entail of persecution Paul suffered, because some had inferred that he had brought a Gentile into the temple (cf. Acts 21:22-29). But no barriers will be found in the New Jerusalem.

13. The absence of sin and presence of the redeemed. 21:27.

27. Sin in all its hideous forms will be entirely excluded. The never-ending beauties of the New Jerusalem are indescribable, but they are such because of the Lord Jesus and His presence there.

16 The Paradise of God

Chapter 22

Apparently, the scene is shifted from the New Jerusalem above the earth to heaven itself. This chapter reveals beautifully that what was lost in Genesis is regained in the Revelation, a true "Paradise Regained."

A. The River of the Water of Life. 22:1.

1. The river, flowing from the throne of God and of the Lamb, speaks of fullness of refreshment, life, and joy (cf. Ps 36:8). In Genesis the tree of life was mentioned first; here the river of life is referred to first. There are heavenly and earthly streams of blessing: earthly in Ezekiel 47:1 and Zechariah 14:8; heavenly in this passage. All comes from the seat of His blessed government.

B. The Tree of Life. 22:2.

2. Satisfying fruit will be there in abundance; saints will partake of it. Even the leaves will promote the sustained health of the nations.

C. The Removal of the Curse. 22:3a.

3a. The curse brought on the human family through the disobedience of Adam (cf. Gen 3:14-19; Rom 5:12) will be wiped out completely. It was paid for at Calvary.

D. The Throne of God and of the Lamb. 22:3b.

3b. There can be no curse where the throne of God and of the Lamb exist. These are spiritual irreconcilables of infinite proportions.

E. The Bliss of the Godly. 22:3c, 4.

3c, 4. God's bond-servants will serve Him, an un-sullied, gladsome, eternal service without failure or weariness and with fulness of joy and praise. Many question whether saints in heaven will see God's face. The Scripture here is plain; they assuredly will. Reread Exodus 24:9-11 (a remarkable vignette). Did not John the apostle at the Last Supper lie on Christ's bosom, hear His heart beat, and look into His face? Cf. John 13:23. Was it not this same beloved disciple that bore witness of what he had heard, seen with his eyes, and handled with his hands, even the Word of Life (cf. 1 Jn 1:1)? But, someone says, mortal man cannot look upon the face of God. This can be true of man in his sinful state and in his condition before his resurrection. But when glorified with the Saviour, it will be entirely different (cf. Rom 8:28-30). In eternity there will always be a difference between deity and redeemed humanity, but this truth does not preclude the "beatific vision," as it has been called. The name of God on the forehead indicates public acknowledgement of belonging to Him, as well as conformity to His blessed nature.

F. The Absence of Darkness. 22:5a, b.

5a, b. How early in life does a child learn fear of darkness; in advanced age it appears again (cf. Eccl 12:1-5). For the believer darkness will be banished forever. Darkness always flees in the presence of light (cf. Jn 1:5). God and Christ are the eternal light of the world.

G. The Saints' Reign. 22:5c.

5c. The millennial reign and the eternal reign are united. Saints will never cease to reign, as long as there will be subjects. Cf. Romans 5:17. Why do earthly reigns come to an end? They are terminated either by injustices, fraud, ineptitude, or death. None of these will be present when Christ the King reigns with His Bride. Why, then, should not the millennial phase of His reign merge into the eternal phase? Verily, it will!

H. The Validity of the Message. 22:6.

6. In a sense this text is a recapitulation of 1:1. If any questioner thinks these disclosures are too good to be authentic, let him now hear yet another confirmation of their reliability and truth.

I. The Coming of Christ. 22:7a.

7a. The soon-coming, without delay, of the Lord Jesus is stated in this chapter three times, verses 7, 12, 20. This is a neat tying in at this point of the end of the book with the beginning (cf. 1:3). After all, this is the dominant theme of the book: the coming revelation of the Lord Jesus (cf. 1:7).

J. The Blessedness of the Obedient. 22:7b.

7b. Blessedness is promised those who treasure, preserve, and live in the light of this prophetic book.

K. John's Reaction to the Revelation. 22:8, 9.

1. His reception of the messages. 22:8a.

2. His worship of the interpreting angel. 22:8b.

3. The angel's warning and advice. 22:9.

8, 9. Again, John, because of the surpassing wonder of the disclosures he has witnessed and heard, seeks to worship the creature who mediated these truths to him. Worship of the creature (cf. 19:10) rather than the Creator is *never* justified (cf. Rom 1:25). The more seemingly worthy the creature, the greater is the danger.

L. The Angel's Final Words. 22:10-19.

1. Book to remain unsealed. 22:10.

10. Contrast these instructions with those of Daniel 12:4. In Daniel the time was far off; here it is near (cf. 1:3).

2. The irreversible states of the ungodly and godly. 22:11.

11. No one will be so foolish as to understand this verse as an invitation to pursue ungodliness. Actually,

there are more exhortations in the text to godliness than
the reverse. The passage is stating that character tends
to become fixed and unchangeable. The common saying is
true: "Sow a thought and reap an act. Sow an act and reap
a habit. Sow a habit and reap a character. Sow a character
and reap a destiny." As one is found in that day, so will he
be eternally. Death or the coming of the Lord fixes
character and eternal destiny.

3. Christ's coming with His rewards. 22:12.

12. For the saints the rewards will be at the judgment seat of Christ. For the nations it will be at the judgment of Matthew 25:31-46. For the wicked dead there will
be no rewards at the Great White Throne.

4. His eternal character. 22:13.

13. As though to intimate the blessed Trinity, there
is a threefold declaration of the eternality of God.

5. The blessedness of the redeemed. 22:14.

14. The AV has unhappily utilized a Greek text here
that is faulty and teaches what the rest of the Bible
denies, that is, salvation by keeping the commandments.
Salvation is rather by symbolically washing their robes in
the blood of the Lamb (cf. 7:14).

6. The ungodly excluded. 22:15.

15. There is always need to warn the unbelieving of
the gravity of their condition. Those excluded are in the
same company as the ones designated in 21:8.

7. The Authenticator of the book. 22:16.

16. Here is a reminder that the message of the book
is for the churches, yet how they have neglected this very
message! The Root connects Christ with Israel and David
(cf. Rom 1:3); the Morning Star (cf. II Pet 1:19) links Him
with the church. The Old Testament ends with Christ as
the Sun of Righteousness (cf. Mal 4:2) to rise with healing
in His wings in millennial blessing; the New Testament
closes with Him as the bright Morning Star. He will come

for His saints before He comes with them to reign, just as the morning star appears before the sun.

    8. Invitation to the unsaved. 22:17.

    17. There are actually three invitations in this important text. The Bible will not close before an opportunity is given to the unsaved to trust Christ. The first two invitations are for the coming of the Lord, although they may be interpreted as a call from the Spirit and the church to the unsaved. The third is clearly for the sinner to come and partake of life in Christ.

    9. Warnings against tampering with the prophecy. 22:18, 19.

    18, 19. The message of the Bible is complete and needs no collaboration from anyone. Here is a most solemn warning which is true of all the Word of God (cf. Deut 12:32), but especially here. What a rebuke to those who treat the message carelessly. There is too much at stake here.

M. The Testimony of Christ to His Coming. 22:20.

    20. "These things" refer to the contents of the entire book; all the message is from Christ personally. He has promised to come quickly (cf. Heb 10:37). If the reckoning were on God's chronometer, hardly two days are gone (cf. II Pet 3:8). The answer of John represents that of the church. Thank God, more are saying it than ever before.

N. Benediction. 22:21.

    21. The Old Testament closed with a threatened curse (cf. Mal 4:6); the New Testament concludes with a benediction of grace. There is this vast difference, because Christ has come and died.

BIBLIOGRAPHY

General Works

Abbott-Smith, G. *A Manual Greek Lexicon of the New Testament.* Edinburgh: T. & T. Clark, 1950.

Aland, K., M. Black, B. M. Metzger, and A. Wikgren. *The Greek New Testament.* London: United Bible Societies, 1966.

Arndt, William F. and F. Wilbur Gingrich. *A Greek-English Lexicon of the New Testament.* Cambridge: The University Press, and Chicago: The University of Chicago Press, 1960.

Brown, F., S. R. Driver, and C. A. Briggs. *A Hebrew and English Lexicon of the Old Testament.* Oxford: Clarendon Press, 1952.

Guthrie, Donald. *New Testament Introduction.* Downers Grove: Inter-Varsity Press, 1975.

Harris, R. L., G. L. Archer, and B. K. Waltke, eds., *Theological Wordbook of the Old Testament.* 2 Volumes. Chicago: Moody Press, 1980.

Koehler, Ludwig and Walter Baumgartner. *Lexicon in Veteris Testamenti Libros.* Grand Rapids: Wm. B. Eerdmans Publishing Company, 1951.

Liddell, H. G. and R. Scott. *A Greek-English Lexicon.* 2 Volumes. Oxford: Clarendon Press, 1948.

Moffatt, James. *The Expositor's Greek Testament.* Volume 5. Grand Rapids: Wm. B. Eerdmans Publishing Company, n.d.

Robertson. A. T. *Word Pictures in the New Testament.* Volume 6. New York: Harper and Brothers Publishers, 1933.

Thiessen, Henry C. *Introduction to the New Testament.* Grand Rapids: Wm. B. Eerdmans Publishing Company, 1943.

Webster's Third New International Dictionary. 3 Volumes. Chicago: G. & C. Merriam Co., 1976.

Young, Robert. *Analytical Concordance to the Bible.* New York: Funk & Wagnalls Company, 22nd ed. rev., n.d.

Combined Work

Beasley-Murray, G. R., H. H. Hobbs, and R. F. Robbins. *Revelation: Three Viewpoints.* Nashville: Broadman Press, 1977.

Amillennial Works

Barclay, William. *The Revelation of John.* 2 Volumes. Philadelphia: Westminster Press, 1961.

Charles, R. H., *A Critical and Exegetical Commentary on The Revelation of St. John.* (International Critical Commentary). 2 Volumes. Edinburgh: T. & T. Clark, 1959.

Hendriksen, W. *More Than Conquerors.* Grand Rapids: Baker Book House, 1981.

Kuyper, Abraham. *The Revelation of St. John.* Grand Rapids: Wm. B. Eerdmans Publishing Co., 1964.

Lenski, R. C. H. *The Interpretation of St. John's Revelation.* Columbus: The Wartburg Press, 1943.

Morris, Leon. *The Revelation of St. John.* Grand Rapids: Wm. B. Eerdmans Publishing Co., 1969.

Pieters, A. *The Lamb, The Woman, and The Dragon.* Grand Rapids: Zondervan Publishing House, 1937.

Premillennial Works

Alford, Henry. *The Greek Testament.* 4 Volumes. (Revelation in Volume 4, Part II.) London: Rivington, 1866.

Criswell, W. A. *Expository Sermons on Revelation.* Grand Rapids: Zondervan Publishing House, 1962.

Gaebelein, A. C. *The Revelation.* New York: "Our Hope," 1915.

Grant, F. W. *The Prophetic History of the Church.* New York: Loizeaux Brothers, n.d.

_____, *The Revelation of Christ.* New York: Loizeaux Brothers, n.d.

Ironside, H. A. *Lectures on the Book of Revelation.* New York: Loizeaux Bros., 1930.

Kelly, W. *Lectures on The Book of Revelation.* London: G. Moorish, n.d.

Lincoln, W. *Lectures on the Book of the Revelation.* New York: Fleming H. Revell Co., n.d.

Newell, William R. *The Book of The Revelation.* Chicago: Grace Publications, Inc., 1939.

Ottman, Ford C. *The Unfolding of the Ages in The Revelation of John.* Grand Rapids: Kregel Publications, 1967.

Pettingill, William L. *The Unveiling of Jesus Christ.* Findlay: Fundamental Truth Publishers, 1939.

Ryrie, Charles C. *Revelation.* Chicago: Moody Press, 1968.

Scott, Walter. *Exposition of the Revelation of Jesus Christ.* London: Pickering & Inglis, n.d.

Seiss, J. A. *The Apocalypse.* Complete in one volume, Philadelphia: Approved Books Store, 15th ed., n.d.

Stevens, W. C. *Revelation, the Crown-Jewel of Biblical Prophecy.* 2 Volumes. Harrisburg: The Christian Alliance Publishing Company, 1928.

Talbot, Louis T. *The Revelation of Jesus Christ.* Los Angeles: the author, 1937.

Thiessen, Henry C. Unpublished Class-notes. Dallas, Texas, n.d.

Walvoord, John F. *The Revelation of Jesus Christ.* Chicago Moody Press, 1966.

INDEX

SUBJECTS

PLACES

SCRIPTURE

Dr. Charles Lee Feinberg is Dean Emeritus of Talbot Theological Seminary.

He was born and reared in Pittsburgh, Pennsylvania, in an orthodox Jewish home, and studied for 14 years preparing for the rabbinate. After his conversion, he received the Th.D. degree from Dallas Theological Seminary and his Ph.D. degree from Johns Hopkins University.

Dr. Feinberg is well-known throughout the world as an outstanding authority on Judaism, and is a popular Bible conference speaker and lecturer. He is the author of 11 books, is a contributor of articles to *Moody Monthly, Bibliotheca Sacra* and other publications, and has written portions of the *IVCF Bible Dictionary, Wycliffe Bible Encyclopedia* and *Commentary,* and the *Zondervan Bible Encyclopedia.* He serves on the Scripture Translation Committee of the Lockman Foundation and for 12 years was a member of the Scofield Reference Bible Revision Committee.